The Curé of Ars
Patron Saint of Parish Priests

"*The good shepherd giveth his life for his sheep.*"   —John 10:11

D0089472

A lithography portrait of the Curé of Ars—St. John Vianney—made in 1845 by the printer Jules Meunier, when the Curé would have been 59 years old.

The Curé of Ars
Patron Saint of Parish Priests

by

Fr. Bartholomew J. O'Brien

"He shall feed his flock like a shepherd: he shall gather together the lambs with his arm, and shall take them up in his bosom, and he himself shall carry them that are with young."
—Isaias 40:11

TAN BOOKS AND PUBLISHERS, INC.
Rockford, Illinois 61105

Nihil Obstat: Francis R. Davis
                  Censor Deputatus

Imprimatur: ✚ James E. Kearney
                  Bishop of Rochester
                  Rochester, August 9, 1956
                  The Feast of St. John Marie Vianney

The Nihil Obstat and Imprimatur are official declarations
that a book or pamphlet is free of doctrinal or moral error.
No implication is contained therein that those who have
granted the Nihil Obstat and Imprimatur agree with the
contents, opinions or statements expressed.

The cover photograph is a picture of the statue sculpted by
Cabuchet, a friend of the Curé of Ars. The statue can be
seen at Ars in a shrine paid for by donations from the priests
of France. Photograph: Xavier Mappus, Lyon.

Library of Congress Catalog Card No.: 87-50942

ISBN: 0-89555-324-4

Printed and bound in the United States of America.

TAN BOOKS AND PUBLISHERS, INC.
P.O. Box 424
Rockford, Illinois 61105

1987

Dedicated to
OUR LADY OF ARS,
of whom the Curé said:
"No grace comes from Heaven
without passing through her hands."

Decree of Pope Pius XI

". . .We are asked by the Bishop of Belley, in whose diocese Ars is located, and in the name of almost 400 archbishops and bishops from all parts of the world, to designate St. John Baptist Vianney as heavenly patron of those who have the care of souls in every location worldwide. Nothing seems more appropriate than to highlight to the parish priests of the world the example of this holy man whom the Church highly praises as outstanding in fulfilling the parochial ministry. . . .Considering the requests of so many bishops and their continued petitions in this year of Our fiftieth priestly ordination anniversary, We think it well to grant their request. Having consulted Camillo Cardinal Laurenti, Prefect of the Sacred Congregation of Rites, by Our own authority and with certain knowledge and full consent, in virtue of Our fullness of Apostolic authority, by this letter We declare and establish St. John Baptist Vianney, Confessor, who was so outstanding and apostolic a man as pastor of the town of Ars, as heavenly patron of all parish priests or those having the care of souls, throughout the whole world. . . .

"Given at Rome by the Holy Father, under the Fisherman's ring, this 23rd day of April, 1929, in the eighth year of Our Pontificate.

"P. Cardinal Gasparri,
Secretary of State"

Words of Pope Pius XI

". . . If, however, your work is to be blessed by God and produce abundant fruit, it must be rooted in holiness of life. Sanctity, as We said above, is the chief and most important endowment of the Catholic priest. Without it other gifts will not go far; with it, even supposing other gifts be meager, the priest can work marvels. We have the example of St. Joseph of Cupertino and, in times nearer to our own, of the humble Curé d'Ars, St. John Mary Vianney, of whom We have already spoken; whom We have willed to set up before all parish priests as their model and heavenly patron."

—from encyclical *Ad Catholici Sacerdotii*
"On the Catholic Priesthood"
Given at Rome, at St. Peter's
December 20, 1935

The Purpose of this Biography

To give to English readers a *concise biography* of the Curé of Ars.

To present as many *facts* (and as few generalities) as possible concerning this saintly priest.

To assemble the *dates* of all the important events in the life of St. John Marie.

To weave into this biography a number of well-known, beautiful *quotations* of the Curé of Ars.

To give in one complete chapter an *overall picture* of each major undertaking of Father Vianney.

To diffuse among the *laity* a wider knowledge of the Patron Saint of Parish Priests.

To offer *priests, seminarians,* and *others* the wonderful events of a life that will *inspire them with zeal for perfection.*

To introduce *five inspiring prints* of M. Cabuchet's famous statue of St. John Marie, found in the Chapel of the Heart of the Curé of Ars, and reproduced with the express permission of the present Curé of Ars, who reserves all rights to these pictures. The photography is the work of "M. Lescuyer et Fils," Lyons, France.

Contents

Mappus/Lescuyer

"You have shown me the way to Ars; I will show you the way to Heaven," the Curé of Ars told young Antoine Givre in February, 1818, when the boy gave him directions how to get to Ars. Young Givre was the first parishioner St. John Vianney met as he approached the town. The picture above is of a monument on the spot where the meeting took place.

Chapter 1

Birth

THE FIRST saint to come to the Vianney home was St. Joseph Benedict Labre. In July, 1770, having just forsaken the *life* of a Trappist to embrace the *spirit* of a Trappist as a wandering mendicant, he had come in holy poverty to beg a night's lodging with the Vianneys. Under his arm he had a Breviary, a Gospel book, and the *Imitation of Christ*. He also had Our Lady's rosary. He was welcomed with the warmest charity and was given a bowl of steaming soup, together with a farmer's supper and the friendship of the whole family. During the evening, one of the Vianney boys, Matthew, watched this meek and humble guest tell and retell his rosary until after family prayers, when he was shown his thick bed of straw over the bakery. St. Joseph Benedict wrote but little. But the Vianney charity so tenderly moved his heart that he later wrote the family a treasured thank-you note. Little did the good saint realize that he had been selected as a kind of precursor for the coming of the saint of this story.

The second saint to come to the Vianney home was the saint of this story, John Marie. He was the son of young Matthew Vianney, who had grown up and married Marie Beluse. John Marie was born about midnight on May 8, 1786, in the family home at Dardilly, France, and was baptized almost immediately. Matthew and Marie Vianney had a family of six children, each of whom was dedicated to Our Blessed Mother while their mother was still carrying them beneath her heart: Catherine, who died shortly after her marriage; Jeanne Marie, who died at the age of five; Francis, who inherited the family home; John Marie, who became our beloved Curé of Ars; Marguerite, who died in 1877 at the age of ninety-one; and Cadet, who joined the army and never returned.

Dardilly is so small a village that it is hardly found on the map. Perhaps in the days of the Vianney family, it had a thousand souls. Some five miles to the southeast was the great city of Lyons. Around the village were farmlands where Matthew Vianney worked, where his sheep and cows grazed, and where a living was made for the family. Dardilly was one of those quiet little Catholic villages of France where the Angelus bell rang, and where people were poor, and where nothing grew as abundantly as the peace in their simple hearts.

While peace blessed the village of Dardilly, the French Revolution rocked the city of Paris. 1789 marked the fall of the Bastille, the symbol of tyranny; 1791 saw the formulation of the Civil Constitution of the Clergy; 1793 inaugurated the infamous Reign of Terror. But the Revolution did not stop at Paris. Its rumblings reverberated in almost every cranny and nook of France, even on to Lyons where the guillotine kept sending souls to eternity without interruption. A price was on the head of every priest. Church bells were silenced, and wayside shrines were toppled over in the grass.

Nevertheless, in Dardilly, seven-year-old John Marie day by day drove the donkey, the cows, and the sheep down into the valley to graze, taking with him his rosary and his small wooden statue of Our Lady. Along the stream there was an old willow tree with a hollow trunk. It was a natural altar. There John Marie placed his Blessed Mother and adorned her with moss, flowers and leaves, and then knelt for his prayers and his Rosaries. Maybe the churches were closed, but surely the soldiers would never find his shrine. If other children came along, he would tie two sticks together into a cross and have a procession—a few hymns would be sung, always a Rosary, and then a sermon (a short one, because his "congregation" would sometimes get restless). But of all this, the leaders of the Revolution never knew.

To strike at the very sources of such religious fervor, the radicals of the Revolution had decreed strong measures against priests. For those who dared to harbor a priest, deportation was the punishment. Matthew Vianney harbored enough priests to have a deportation to the moon. At times, Holy Mass was celebrated in his home. At other times, young John Marie and the family would set out at night in great silence for some barn in the neighborhood where Holy Mass would be offered by a hunted priest. There in the darkness and the bareness of a barn would be found a candle, a plain table, and the necessities for the Holy Sacrifice. The mystery of everything—the whispers, the sobs, the breathing, and the sighs—so moved the boy that his soul was no doubt made most receptive to the vocational whisperings of the Holy Spirit. During those days, he experienced the fear, the mystery and the faith of the catacombs; in his memory, the days of the Terror were ever strong.

Little did the French Revolutionaries dream that they would forge in the fire of their hate, on the anvil of their persecution, a saint who would bring back to France the very God they had vowed to destroy.

CHAPTER 2

Boyhood

JOHN MARIE was not a dull child. Because the school in Dardilly had been closed, he had no chance to get an education. His elder sister, Catherine, tried to fill this void by teaching him to read, to write, and to spell the words of a prayer book. Fortunately, early in 1795, a school was opened and John Marie was permitted to attend—at least until the planting days of springtime. He must have done well in history, geography, and the three R's because citizen Dumas, the master of the school, used to say to the other students, "Oh! if you were like little Vianney!"

In 1797 Father Groboz, who had been concealing his identity during the Revolution by acting as a cook, stopped at the house of the Vianneys and met John Marie.

"How old are you, John?" the priest inquired.

"Eleven, Father."

"And how long has it been since you last went to confession?"

"Father, I have never gone to confession."

"Then, John my boy," answered the priest without hesitation, "right here and now you will make your first confession."

5

There in his own home, beneath the old family clock, John Marie knelt and revealed his soul in his first confession. He had little of sin to tell the priest because in years to come he was heard to say, "I knew nothing of evil until I learned to know it in the confessional."

John Marie's first Holy Communion was postponed until he was thirteen years old—until May of 1798. For his preparation he went to Ecully, a village on the road to Lyons about three miles from Dardilly, and lived at the home of his Aunt Marguerite Humbert. In Ecully, two Sisters of St. Charles were holding classes secretly to instruct children for their first Holy Communion. These classes John Marie attended and diligently prepared to receive for the first time his Eucharistic Master.

In the private home of Madame de Pingon, John Marie, together with fifteen other children, was to receive his first Holy Communion. The memorable day arrived, classes were over, and well-planned precautions had been made to hide the event from the crafty eyes of the Revolutionaries. Very early in the morning, the children gathered together in their old clothes, except for a veil or an armlet which the mothers had hidden beneath their capes. Outside the house, the men had placed wagons of hay (which they were actually unloading) in order to block off the windows and conceal the lighted candles the little communicants were to carry. One by one, the children were directed into a large room where the shutters were drawn and where a hunted priest was to offer the Holy Sacrifice of the Mass. There, in the presence of a few and with the simplicity of the catacombs, John Marie received his first Holy Communion. "I was present," his sister Marguerite related many years later, "and my brother felt such happiness that he was unwilling to leave the room." John Marie was given a plain rosary in memory of the occasion, and this he still treasured fifty years later. But the day came to an end, and with the day, there also came to an end his time of boyhood and of study. He went back home with his mother and father. It was springtime, and there was work to be done.

Over the years, there was much work to be done: haying, harvesting, and gathering of the grapes and the apples and the other fruits. The stables had to be cleaned; the fields had to be ploughed; the grapes had to be pressed; and the trees had to be pruned for a better harvest. "Oh, what a beautiful thing it is," he used to say in later years, "to offer oneself each morning as a victim to God! Oh what a beautiful thing it is to do all things in union with the good God!"

In the early dawn of April 18, 1802, the glorious Feast of Easter, the giant bell of Notre Dame in Paris rang out and proclaimed the spiritual resurrection of the Catholic Church in France. John Marie shed tears when the news reached Dardilly. Soon the church doors opened and the great bells pealed. More important still, to the nearby village of Ecully came Father Balley, the priest who was to prove so helpful to John Marie.

All this time, the vocation to the priesthood was becoming more and more attractive to John Marie. At night, he used to stay up and read by the light of a rosin candle the Gospels or the *Imitation of Christ*. His soul was indeed ripe for the seminary; but his mind, at seventeen, had hardly received the seedlings of elementary studies. He knew no Latin. To make things more difficult, Francis was to be drafted; and Catherine was to be married, and Mr. Vianney had to provide a dowry. "If I were a priest," he confided to his mother, "I should gain many souls to God." The guillotine had robbed France of many of her priests, and France needed priests.

For years, John Marie's father said a definite "No" to any permissions to study for the priesthood. In conscience, the father honestly believed he could not spare the boy. He too wanted to do God's holy will; and undoubtedly he did, because those teen years which John Marie spent in Dardilly were like the hidden years which Jesus spent in Nazareth. It was the mother who pleaded for her son. Father Balley was opening up a minor seminary in his rectory at Ecully, and John Marie could study there and still not be far from the farm. Besides, he could live once again at the house of Aunt Marguerite, and it would not cost much. "Very well," agreed the father. "Since the boy has his heart on this thing, we cannot oppose him any longer."

John Marie was nineteen years old when he

bade farewell to the fields and his home at Dardilly. His mother went with him to Ecully, where the austere Father Balley greeted him and reassured him with these fatherly words: "Do not worry, my friend. If need be, I will sacrifice myself for your sake."

CHAPTER 3

Service

JOHN MARIE entered the seminary, or rather, the rectory school of Father Balley, a learned man who had repeatedly declined the chair of moral theology at the major seminary of Lyons. John Marie entered the small school, and progressed sadly—not that he lacked the ability to learn, but that he had missed the opportunities to have studied. The two other pupils used to snicker and giggle upon hearing this big farmer blunder through lessons that they had learned with ease. In fact, John's apparent stupidity was too great for one of the students, Mathias Loras. He literally threw up his hands in disgust. Seeing this, John Marie knelt down before this boy of twelve and begged forgiveness. Mathias' heart was of gold; and being grieved, he threw himself into the arms of his husky confrere and wept like a child. This boy was to become the great and pious Bishop Loras who died in America, February 19, 1858, as the Bishop of Dubuque, Iowa.

Not understanding the grammar of his native language, John Marie found it next to impossible to learn the grammar of Latin. Temptations swooped down upon him in the way of discouragement. Was he undertaking too much? Was he tempting God in wanting to be a priest? He confided to Father Balley, "I want to go home." But this would mean not to labor for souls! So the good God came to the rescue of His seminarian and inspired him to undertake a pilgrimage to the shrine of St. Francis Regis some sixty-two miles away to seek the holy will of God in regard to his vocation.

In the summer of 1806, the young seminarian set out, with a stick in one hand, a rosary in the other, and a vow in his heart to beg his way to the shrine. At a house where he stopped to beg for bread, a woman asked him to help her unwind a ball of thread. Having helped the woman with her spinning, John Marie went to the door for the food his service had merited, only to find it slammed in his face. After many like disappointments, he finally arrived at the shrine and prayed for "grace to learn enough Latin to enable him to do his theology." Grace was granted to him; from then on, no discouragement would prevent his progress in study, even though the progress was little and greatly interrupted. During the return journey, he was advised in confession to practice the words of Holy Scripture: "It is more blessed to give than to receive." And so it was that John Marie returned to Ecully, giving alms—the money he had carried for his journey— to the needy he met on the way.

Progress in studies was to be slow indeed for John Marie; and he was to need, sorely indeed, every grace that St. Francis Regis had won for him. To strengthen him for the trials to come, he received in 1807 the Sacrament of Confirmation from Cardinal Fesch, Archbishop of Lyons and uncle of the Emperor Napoleon. As his Confirmation patron saint he chose the Precursor, John the Baptist.

Two years of peace followed—then came the blow. In the autumn of 1809, a police officer from Lyons appeared at the Vianney farm in Dardilly. His mission: to draft John Marie Vianney into the armies of Napoleon.

Certain concessions had been made by the Emperor to exempt seminarians from military service. But in 1809, Napoleon was hard pressed. France's manpower had been depleted; the War Office needed men—any man, provided he could at least walk. Father Balley had written to the chancery office of Lyons, but the supreme appeal on the seminarian's behalf came too late. Nothing could be done. John Marie was to report for duty at the military depots of Lyons.

October 26, 1809, found John Marie in army barracks. He was galled by what he heard and saw. But in obedience, he unflinchingly submitted to the hardships of military training. However, after two days of training, because of his studies and penances at Ecully, his strength failed. An army physician ordered him to the hospital.

On November 12, John Marie was still convalescing, but nevertheless he was judged strong enough to join the draft leaving Lyons for Roanne. He rode along in some kind of conveyance; but suffering from the cold due to his lack of military clothing, he had a serious relapse which hospitalized him again, this time in Roanne.

On January 5, 1810, Infantryman Vianney was ordered to join a detachment of soldiers setting out on the morrow for the Spanish frontier. John Marie said farewell to the kind sisters who had cared for him at the hospital and started out in sufficient time to join his regiment. On his way, however, he stopped at a church to pay Jesus a visit—but with Jesus, time does not exist, and after a visit which seemed too short but which proved too long, John Marie missed his regiment.

The young soldier reported to his superior officer the next morning. In no certain words, the officer growled: "Get going. Catch up with the rearguard. Do you want gendarmes and chains?" Weak and sick in body, he set out alone. His sack seemed to weigh tons. He prayed his Rosary as he had never prayed it before. He had confidence in Our Lady. He asked her to help him. Then suddenly, a stranger appeared and asked: "What are you doing here? Come with me!"

The stranger (a man named Guy, who later proved to be a deserter) picked up the sack and started off. John Marie, weary and confused, followed him up the tree-clad side of a mountain until they came to the tiny village of Les Noes.

"You can hide in our village, which is completely surrounded by forests."

"Oh no!" replied John Marie. "My parents have

been sufficiently worried as it is."

"Do not let that trouble you. There are already a good many in hiding in these parts."

What was John Marie to do? At least for the night he had to stay someplace. So he left himself in the hands of Divine Providence. He was given some food. Then, faint from the day's experience, he sank into a deep sleep in the house of one of Guy's friends up beyond the village. The next morning he woke up only to find himself a *deserter*, since he was advised of the absolute impossibility of ever catching up with the rearguard, even with the best will in the world. Comte des Garets later was to sum up this crisis in this way: "Unpremeditated circumstances brought it about that Father Vianney found himself a deserter." Because of such circumstances, in later life Father Vianney never accused himself of sin in regard to his so-called desertion.

John Marie found a friend in the Mayor of Les Noes, who was opposed to the government of Napoleon. The mayor changed John Marie's name to Jerome Vincent, declared him to be a cousin, and sent him to live with his relative, a widow and a mother of four children, by the name of Claudine Fayot. She lived a short distance above the village in a tiny hamlet called Les Robins. Everyone spoke of Claudine as Mother Fayot, and it was not long before she became a second mother to John Marie. Here he remained two years, hiding in the stable by day, teaching the children by night, away from his family, away from his studies, and away from even Holy Mass. The gendarmes used to come, and

John Marie would bury himself in the hay. Once, in poking through the hay, a gendarme speared him with his sword, but God protected his servant and saved him for greater things.

On April 2, 1810, Napoleon married the Archduchess Marie-Louise, and the occasion was marked by a general pardon of all deserters. The farewell of their "dear cousin" from the village in January, 1811, was one of tender sorrow. How they loved their Jerome Vincent! So sure were they that God had destined him for the priesthood, that before his departure the good people brought him a cassock and made him wear it for an hour or so just to see what he would look like in the days to come.

John Marie arrived home in time to enjoy the company of his mother for a little while; for soon he was to help her to go to God for her eternal reward. In years to come, John Marie would never speak of his mother but with tears. When he lost her, he lost all attachment to the things of time. All his life, like the great Augustine, he remembered her—his most precious advocate—at the altar.

CHAPTER 4

Seminary

THE CHURCH of France was desperate for priests. Therefore, the strict Canonical laws pertaining to candidates had to be set aside to meet the emergency. The Cardinal of Lyons was satisfied with one year of philosophy and only two years of theology. "We must go to the rescue of many parishes left entirely without priests," he wrote to his Vicar General, Father Courbon. In fact, in 1812, His Eminence called to Holy Orders all those who were in their first year of theology in order to guard them from the danger of conscription. On one point only was he inflexible—piety.

Following his mother's death, John Marie was welcomed back to the rectory of Father Balley, where he acted as student, gardener, sacristan, altar boy and domestic helper. In the diocese of Lyons, tonsure was given to students in the minor seminary during the year of rhetoric. Father Balley realized that time was pressing and that his seminarian was twenty-four years old. Therefore, he presented John Marie, while a student of rhetoric, for tonsure, on May 28, 1811. On that happy day, John Marie took the first step in his ecclesiastical career towards the priesthood.

In the history of John Marie, the role that God chose for Father Balley in leading him to the priesthood and in forming him into a saint is most remarkable. A parishioner described Father Balley in this way: "He was a tall man, made apparently of nothing but skin and bones. One might have thought that he never ate a square meal." His pupil set out to follow in the penitential footsteps of this holy priest, and if possible, to outstep him in the path to perfection. Father Balley felt so strongly that John Marie was called to the holy priesthood that he never once grew weary in his efforts to promote his vocation.

In 1812, Father Balley sent his pupil to study philosophy at the minor seminary of Verrieres. There, John found himself older than the other students, even older than his professor. A few of his fellow students were hardly more advanced than he, so a group of seven of them was taken aside and taught philosophy in French. While in the minor seminary he dedicated himself to Our Lady as her slave according to the mind of St. Louis De Montfort. In spite of the fact that he was often made the butt of his fellow seminarians when he was in the philosophy class, he nevertheless was well-liked and considered already very close to God. In later life, he summed up his stay at Verrieres by the simple, charitable remark, "I had somewhat to suffer."

After a very pleasant summer vacation with Father Balley, John Marie entered the major

seminary of St. Irénée at Lyons in October, 1813.
He was looked upon as a saint—but his lack of
knowledge in Latin was his stumbling block. One
of his fellow students said years later: "The result of his studies was *nil*, the cause being his
inadequate knowledge of Latin. More than once
I explained things to him, but he did not seem
able to grasp them. His application, nevertheless,
was unfailing." The term examinations came up.
John Marie failed. The authorities considered the
situation, and John Marie was asked to leave.
Around Easter of 1814 he left St. Irénée and
returned to his good friend, Father Balley, in order
to complete his theological studies in French. Fac-
ing facts as they were, he thought perhaps God
wished him to enter the Brotherhood. But Father
Balley quickly put an end to such thoughts, and
the two of them had recourse to prayer—and then
to the textbooks.

Hardly three months after his dismissal from
the major seminary, his good pastor sent John
Marie back to the seminary to take his canoni-
cals for Minor Orders. But he was so overawed
by the venerable jury and their Latin questions
that he became all confused and the verdict was,
"Unsatisfactory!"

The next day, Father Balley set out for Lyons
and went directly to the chancery office. He spoke
of his high esteem for his pupil and begged for
another examination. In his great charity, the
Vicar-General not only granted another examination but promised to come with the superior

of the major seminary to Ecully and question John
Marie at the rectory in his own familiar surround-
ings. As a result, John Marie gave very good and
satisfactory answers to all the questions put to
him.

The final decision rested with the first Vicar
General, Father Courbon, who was directing the
diocese in the absence of the Cardinal. (His Eminence had to leave the diocese in a hurry following the Emperor's abdication.) Father Courbon
was a simple priest and a good priest, and he
asked in great sincerity:

"Is the young Vianney pious?"

"Oh yes!"

"Has he a devotion to Our Lady?"

"Oh yes!"

"Does he know how to say his Rosary?"

"Oh yes! He is a model of piety."

"A model of piety!" repeated the Vicar General.
"Very well, I shall summon him to come up for
ordination. The grace of God will do the rest."

On the Feast of the Visitation, July 2, 1814,
in the Cathedral of St. Jean in Lyons, John Marie
received Minor Orders and the subdiaconate from
the hands of Bishop Simon, who had come from
Grenoble for the ceremony.

Father Balley had made himself responsible for
his seminarian. Consequently, John Marie was sent
back to Ecully for his final year of theology. This
was most fortunate, because the political spirit
of France had entered the major seminary, and
as a result there was much unrest and even

violence among the students. From this John Marie was spared. In May, 1815, he returned to the seminary to prepare for the diaconate, which he received on June 23 from Bishop Simon in the Cathedral of Lyons.

The holy priesthood was now in sight; the end of the road was near. But there was another canonical examination. It lasted over an hour. This time the result was most satisfactory, and so the date of ordination was set for August 13, 1815. As the Vicar General put his name to the testimonial letters he remarked, "The Church is in need not only of learned priests; she wants, above all, holy priests."

All alone, journeying on foot, John Marie set out for Grenoble some sixty miles away, where Bishop Simon was to ordain him. He carried a small parcel and an alb for his first private Mass. He arrived on Saturday night and presented himself on Sunday morning, the thirteenth Sunday after Pentecost, to the Bishop for ordination to the holy priesthood. He was the only candidate, alone, a stranger in a strange diocese. Excuses were made to the Bishop for troubling him with only one candidate, but the good Bishop smiled and said: "It is not too much trouble to ordain a good priest!" So, at the age of twenty-nine years, in the chapel of the major seminary in Grenoble, John Marie Vianney became Father Vianney, and from that time on, never once did he forget the dignity and the glory of his priesthood. "Oh! how great is the priest," he used to say in later years.

"The priest will only be understood in Heaven. Were he understood on earth, people would die, not of fear, but of love."

The next day, in the same chapel, he offered his first private Mass. And the closest Friend he had with whom to share the joy of his first Mass was Jesus Himself.

Lescuyer

What sweetness do we not find
in forgetting ourselves
in order to seek God!

CHAPTER 5

Assistant

THE SAINTLY Father Balley had trained Father Vianney as a seminarian; now Divine Providence had so arranged that he would also train him as a priest. When Father Vianney reached the rectory at Ecully, and after Father Balley had knelt down for his priestly blessing and had kissed his anointed hands, the venerable old pastor smiled at the young priest and told him the happy news: the Vicar General had given Ecully an assistant, and the assistant was to be none other than Father John Marie himself. The people were as pleased as the pastor. "Father Vianney has edified us during the time he studied here," they said to one another. "What will he not do now that he is a priest?"

From the very first everyone loved Father Vianney. His sister Marguerite went over from Dardilly to hear him preach, and later remarked, "To my thinking, he did not preach well as yet, but when it was his turn to speak, people flocked to the church." He was kept busy, preparing his catechism lessons, looking after the sick (who always seemed to ask for the new assistant), writing his sermons which in the beginning were very short, studying his theology, and working out practical cases of conscience under the direction of his pastor.

Occasionally, pastor and assistant would go on a pilgrimage to the shrine of Our Lady of Fourviére. Or, once in a while, they would visit friends in Lyons, the Loras family or the Jaricot family. It was in this way that Father Vianney met Pauline Jaricot, a young girl of about sixteen, who was destined to do monumental work for the missions. During one of the gatherings at the Jaricot home, the conversation centered on the virgin martyr whose body had recently been found in the catacombs of Rome. It was the first time that Father Vianney had ever heard of his little friend of future years, St. Philomena.

The rectory at Ecully was a kind of Trappist monastery where the two priests lived in common and in great peace, praying together and edifying each other in a kind of holy rivalry. The table was simple: brown bread, potatoes, (no wine), and a piece of beef which eventually turned black from age. But when guests came, things were different.

Father Balley wore a hair-shirt. So, Father Vianney wore a hair-shirt. Father Balley reported Father Vianney to the chancery for being too strict with himself. So, Father Vianney reported Father Balley. And the Vicar General laughed at them both and sent them back to Ecully.

"How is Father Vianney?" asked one of the curate's old comrades of Father Balley.

"Oh," remarked the pastor, "Father Vianney is always the same—he gives away all he possesses."

It was during his stay at Ecully that Father Vianney started his lifelong practice of praying to Our Lady to free him from all sensual temptations. Under vow, he promised to say daily to Our Lady the *Regina Coeli* and to add six times the ejaculation: "Blessed be forever the most holy and Immaculate Conception of the Blessed Virgin Mary, Mother of God. Amen." As a result, he seemed to receive special graces of heroic purity and of seeing everyone without looking at anyone.

But these happy years were soon to end. The early days of the Terror were beginning to tell on Father Balley, although he was only sixty-five years old. In February, 1817, an ulcer formed on his leg. It gradually became gangrenous and eventually forced the doctors to consider his condition hopeless. During the whole of 1817, Father Vianney was doing most of the parish work, besides assisting his pastor as a faithful son would assist his father. December 17, 1817 was the date God chose to call His faithful servant home. Father Balley went to confession to his assistant (whom he had chosen to be his spiritual director and father confessor as soon as faculties had been granted), and received Holy Viaticum and Extreme Unction. He whispered a few words of kindness and advice to his young friend, and then reached under his pillow for something. He wanted his discipline[1] and hair-shirt. "Look, my poor child," whispered the dying priest, "hide these things. If they were found after my death, people would imagine that I have sufficiently expiated my sins, and so they would leave me in Purgatory until the end of the world." Father Vianney took them, but he did not hide them. He used them himself.

"I have seen beautiful souls, but none so beautiful!" said Father Vianney, who wept like a child at the death of his good and faithful fellow priest, Father Balley. It was always with tears that he later spoke of Father Balley. "If I were an artist, I could still paint his portrait." And every day, his name was pronounced by Father Vianney at the memento of the Mass. On his mantelpiece, he always kept the looking glass of his good pastor because "it had reflected his face."

The people petitioned that Father Vianney be their new pastor, but the authorities refused. A new pastor was appointed. Things were different now. He did not care to make the rectory into a monastery, and too, he found the assistant too rigid. Did he ask for another assistant? It is not known for certain.

In the meantime, a young priest of the diocese, Father Deplace, had died. He was only twenty-seven years old and had died of consumption after a ministry of but twenty-three days. His death left open for some weeks a small parish of about two hundred and thirty souls. To this parish Father Vianney was appointed by the Vicar General, who said to him, "There is not much love for God in that parish; you will bring some into it."

On February 9, 1918, Father Vianney set out to become the Curé of Ars.

NOTE

1. A discipline is a scourge by which a person voluntarily beats himself as a penance or mortification in imitation of the whipping of Our Lord at the pillar.

CHAPTER 6

Ars

O N MOST maps of France, the village of Ars is never found. Ars is about twenty-two miles from Lyons, in that part of the diocese which was looked upon as a kind of Siberia. The village was in a forsaken part of France. Even the roads to Ars were bad. A strange air of melancholy brooded over the village.

Nature did but little to grace the countryside of Ars. The soil was poor; the ponds were stagnant; the woods were made up of thickets of bushes. Huddled together were some forty houses, low, drab, and made of clay. Maybe twenty more houses were scattered in the flats beyond the village proper.

In one small section of the village was the church, the rectory, the cemetery, and an orchard of walnut trees. The church, dedicated to St. Sixtus, was small, yellow, and poor, built in an architecture all of its own. The rectory was no more than a peasant's house.

At one end of the village was a chateau owned by a wealthy family by the name of Les Garets. The chateau, with its tower, moat and battlements, made a strange contrast with the rest of the village. Here lived the pious and generous chatelaine, Mademoiselle des Garets, more commonly known as Mademoiselle d'Ars, who, in her deep devotion, recited the Divine Office each day. She and her brother, Vicomte Francis, who was married and who lived in Paris, were most generous to the church.

In spite of the smallness of the village and the poverty of its people, Ars possessed four taverns. Around these centered the social life of the people. As a result, they became worldly minded, pleasure hungry, and in time, weak and indifferent toward their religious practices. Drinking, dancing, rowdyism, mixed with ignorance, weak faith, and a forgetfulness of devotions, made a sorry sight out of Ars. However, Ars was not worse than other villages. The bad effects of the Terror and the Revolution were found throughout France, and few priests remained to teach the people and the children the simple rudiments of their religion.

It is about nineteen miles from Ecully to Ars. Father Vianney walked the distance, together with Mother Bibost, who was to be his housekeeper; and with them went a friend who drove a cart on which were piled an old wooden bedstead, some clothes, and a few books left to Father Vianney by Father Balley. The day was misty, and the travelers became lost. No one seemed able to direct them. On they went, hoping for the best, until, through the haze, they saw some young shepherd children.

"Please, children, where is Ars?" But the

children spoke only a local dialect.

"Ars? Ars?" repeated the Cure. "Where is Ars?"

Finally, a boy, Antoin Givre, understood, and pointed the way.

"My young friend," said Father Vianney, "you have shown me the way to Ars; I shall show you the way to Heaven." And years later, the first one to follow the Curé of Ars to Heaven was indeed Antoin Givre.

Learning they were on the boundary of the parish, the new Curé of Ars got on his knees and prayed in a field before continuing his journey. He was entering his new parish. Did he pray to the guardian angel of the parish, or to St. Sixtus, or perhaps to the Holy Spirit for light and guidance? As he came in sight of the tiny village and saw how small it was, he stopped again, and to himself he whispered, "Yet this parish will not be able to contain the multitude of those who shall journey hither!"

The next morning the Curé of Ars rang the bell for Holy Mass, and then the people knew they had a pastor. But most of them did not seem to care.

On Sunday, February 13, 1818, Father Vianney was properly installed as the pastor of Ars by his neighboring priest, Father Ducreux. Nearly everybody came; the church was full. Everyone was curious to get a look at the new priest. They found that their priest was of medium height, very thin, and somewhat awkward in his manner. They noticed that his cassock was of a coarse material, and that his shoes were poor and rough like their own. When he offered Holy Mass, he seemed different from other priests; there was a spirit of awe and love and reverence that set him apart. Most of the people did not know just what to say when the ceremony of installation was over. But the mayor, Antoine Mandy, summed up the occasion with the simple words, "We have a poor church, but a holy parish priest."

CHAPTER 7

Beginnings

FATHER VIANNEY began his duties as the new pastor by taking a census. (He kept the record of some sixty families in his head.) About noon, when children and parents were certain to be at table, Father Vianney made his visits. He stood at one side of the kitchen (never sitting down to eat) and just passed the time of day asking questions about the crops, the children, and the relatives. Always he finished his brief visit with a word about God and His Church. Day by day, he picked up not only a full acquaintance with each family, but also a full picture of the morality of his parish—and he found the picture blurred and scarred and in great need of restoration.

The new Curé realized the meaning of the words of Jesus to His Apostles: "This kind can only be cast out by prayer and fasting." [*Matt.* 17:20]. Therefore, he would undertake a one-man campaign of prayer and fasting, and win for his people the graces necessary to bring them back to Sunday Mass and to the practice of their religion. He would also win for them the graces demanded to take them away from drinking, from the taverns, from excessive pleasure, blasphemy and impurity. So the campaign for souls was inaugurated by the Curé of Ars, and this personal campaign ended only with his death.

A man who lived near the church wondered what the new Curé was doing in there so very early each morning. One morning, long before dawn, when the man saw a tiny candle making its way from the rectory through the darkness across the cemetery, he sneaked over to the church and peeked in to find out for himself. There was the pastor, pouring out his heart to Jesus hidden in the Blessed Sacrament! "Ah," said the man, "he is not like other men!" What did the Curé say to his blessed Jesus? Henri Ghéon has given us his version of the Curé's prayer. Prostate on the floor or kneeling with outstretched hands, the Curé thus prayed or groaned or wept out his heart:

"My God, my all, You see how I love You, and I do not love You enough.

"My God, You have given me all; behold the little that I give You. Give me the strength to give more.

"My God, here is all—take all; but convert my parish. If You do not convert it, it will be because I have not deserved it.

"My God, I count my merits as nothing, but Yours are infinite. May they win for me the grace of suffering.

"My God, I consent to suffer all that You may wish for all my life...for a hundred years...and the most bitter suffering, but convert them...."

(*The Secret of the Curé D'Ars*, Henri Ghéon, p.53.)

In those early days, often the Curé walked alone out over the countryside, reading his Divine Office or reciting his Rosary. Sometimes his parishioners found him here or there on his knees, perhaps for the *Gloria Patri* of his Office, or the opening or closing prayer. Once, however, Mr. Mandy found him kneeling in a secluded spot and weeping like a child: "My God, convert my parish! My God, convert my parish!" Over and over he pleaded with God. Mr. Mandy left him to his prayer.

If there was need to see the pastor, the parishioners knew where to find him: over in the church. There were days when he left the church only after the evening Angelus.

To his prayer, he added penance. Most people save souls one at a time; Father Vianney saved souls hundreds at a time. The number he saved was in proportion to the price he paid. Was he imprudent in the extreme of his penances? The Church does not call him *imprudent*, but *heroic*, and God blessed his ministry with thousands of souls. However, he himself later remarked, "When one is young, one is apt to be indiscreet."

Shortly after arriving in Ars, the Curé gave his mattress away and slept on the floor, using a log of wood as a pillow. Upon visiting Mlle. d'Ars, he asked her kindly to take back the many things she had previously loaned to the rectory: six high-backed velvet-covered chairs and one armchair to match, another armchair covered with green and red Siam cotton, a quilted coverlet of white and gold taffeta, and other pieces of furniture. He asked, however, for permission to keep some special articles: two old tables, a bookcase, some straw-bottomed chairs and a cast iron saucepan.

Someone has said that a discipline lasted him fifteen days. No wonder! It was lashed against the flesh for at least an hour a night. If this caused blood to flow from his poor body, it also caused grace to flow into his poor soul. He made his own discipline, or at least added to it bits of lead or old keys in order to make it more effective.

Mother Bibost, who had come from Ecully to be housekeeper, was soon demoted to merely *honorary* housekeeper, and finally, her services were really not needed at all. Then Mrs. Renard took over. She was going to have at least fresh bread. But the pastor gave it to the poor. He wanted only a few pancakes and some potatoes every few days or so. No more! Other women tried to help out. One gave up with the sigh, "Oh, it is very hard to serve a saint!"

So once a week Father Vianney cooked for himself a saucepan of potatoes. When hungry, he cooked an egg or made some pancakes. His meals were never at regular intervals. He ate when necessary, but only to keep the body going. This was his manner of life until 1827, when he began to take his meals with the orphans at Providence.

In 1839, a young priest, Father Tailhades, came to spend a few weeks with the Curé of Ars and

to study the apostolic work in country parishes.
To him, the Curé opened up his heart and gave
him these words of advice which give us a glimpse
into his own soul during these early days at Ars:

"My friend, the devil is not greatly afraid of
the discipline and other instruments of penance.
That which beats him is the curtailment of one's
food, drink, and sleep. There is nothing the devil
fears more; consequently, nothing is more pleasing to God. Oh! how often have I experienced
it! While I was alone—and I was alone during
eight or nine years, and therefore quite free to
yield to my attraction—it happened at times that
I refrained from food for entire days. On those
occasions I obtained, both for myself and for
others, whatsoever I asked of Almighty God."

He could not recall these days without tears.
But he continued:

"Now things are not quite the same. I cannot
do without food for so long a time, and if I attempt it, I lose the power even of speech. But
how happy I was while I lived alone! I bought
from the poor the morsels of bread that were given
them; I spent a good part of the night in the
church; there were not so many people to con-
fess, and the good God granted me extraordinary
graces."

Thus did the good Curé of Ars win the graces
which were to reform the village of Ars and win
souls to Christ, the number of which is recorded
only in Heaven.

CHAPTER 8

Reform

THE CURÉ of Ars understood well the powerful words of St. Paul, "Rebuke them sharply that they may be sound in faith." [*Titus* 1:13]. So the Curé began to preach and to catechize in order to awaken the people of Ars from their ignorance and indifference.

The Curé's study was the sacristy, his desk was the vestment case, and his inspiration was the tabernacle a step away. There in the church he studied his books and wrote his sermons, ten or twenty pages long and an hour in length. His library consisted of the Lives of the Saints, the *Catechism of the Council of Trent*, *The Dictionary of Theology*, the spiritual works of Rodriguez, and various sermon books.

Father Vianney read books and then knelt before the altar in order to put his thoughts together. He strove to be simple because his people were simple. Next he stood at the vestment case and wrote and wrote, without paragraphs, and almost without end. But the greatest task of all was memorizing those pages. The night was spent in this. Those who passed by the church could hear him reciting and practicing. It was hard work—

but Ars must be converted!

Sunday morning came, and a few people came, and then came time for the sermon. Sometimes the Curé would forget, or in his efforts, he would lose his voice. He offered the humiliation for his people. But when he did preach, he poured out his sermon in a loud and passionate voice, full of zeal and unction, and usually with tears. Yet, some of the people yawned, and latecomers banged the door.

Father Vianney never ceased to catechize the little children until 1845, when he received an assistant priest. Every answer of the catechism had to be learned word for word, and the best pupil received a holy card. If the children had to work in the fields, then the classes were held as early as six in the morning. The first one to arrive received a prize. Every child was to carry a rosary, and the Curé had a few extra ones in his pocket—just in case. Gradually, a generation of well-instructed Catholic children began to grow up in Ars.

During the Easter season of 1818, Father Vianney discovered that most of the men refused to make their Easter duty. During the summer season, the poor Curé could hear the carts rumbling off to the fields on Sunday morning, and also the anvil striking its loud blows down at the smith's shop. The church had some women, but only a few men. The men worked all day Sunday, then dressed in their best and spent the evening (and most of their money) in one of the four inns, drinking, blaspheming, and exchanging vulgar stories until the early hours of the morning. Had the inns been places of simple amusement, Father Vianney would have said nothing. But it was obvious that they were places of sin. So he struck fearlessly at the innkeepers.

"The innkeepers," he cried out one Sunday at Mass (and the word got back to the innkeepers themselves), "steal the bread of a poor woman and her children by selling wine to drunkards who spend on Sunday what they have earned during the week. If he wishes to escape eternal damnation, a priest may not and cannot absolve innkeepers who, either at night or during church hours, serve those drunkards with wine. Ah! the innkeepers! The devil does not trouble them much; on the contrary, he despises them and spits upon them."

One innkeeper complained that the Curé was completely ruining his business. The Curé gave him some money and prevailed upon him to close his business. He obeyed and eventually became a model Catholic. Others obeyed too, but seven different proprietors opened new taverns. "You shall see, you shall see," warned the Curé, "you shall see that those who open an inn in this parish shall be ruined." He was right, and in time Ars was rid of all taverns. By 1858 there were established five hotels or tourists houses, and the Curé permitted these for the accommodations of the pilgrims. Years later, the schoolmaster, Mr. Pertinand, made this observation: "There were very few destitute persons at Ars itself. By suppressing the taverns, the Curé of Ars had eliminated the main cause of poverty."

Also by suppressing the taverns, the Curé had eliminated the main cause of blasphemy. In time, the people of Ars were known for their reverence for the Holy Name. "How good God is! Blessed be God!" were expressions often heard in the simple conversations of the people.

One Sunday in July, the Curé took a walk along one of the roads close by the church. A parishioner, harvesting his crop, spied the pastor. Embarrassed and ashamed, he tried to hide behind his cart: "O my friend," warned the Curé, "you seem very much surprised to find me here. But the good God sees you at all times. He It is whom you must fear."

Knowing the weakness of his people, the Curé even refused to grant dispensations lest they lead to abuse and carelessness. "Yes," he used to say to those who asked, "elsewhere priests may grant permission to work on Sunday. I, at Ars, cannot do so." This was the firmness which eventually made Sunday at Ars truly the Lord's Day.

But there was one more abuse he endeavored to conquer, and that was the mania for dancing. It cost him the effort of twenty-five years to subdue this passion. Knowing what took place at those dances, he openly spoke out to the parents of the young men and women:

"You must answer for their souls as you will answer for your own. I wonder whether you are doing all that lies in your power. . . .But what I do know is that if your children lose their souls while they are as yet under your care, it is to be feared that your lack of watchfulness may be the cause of your own damnation. . . .I know you will not take another step in order to do your duty to your children; these things do not greatly trouble you, and I should almost say you are right, for you will have plenty of time to worry during the endless eternity."

Once the Curé met the fiddler who was engaged to play at a dance. He learned his price, paid him twice as much, and sent him back home. That night, there was no dance.

God inspires His saints to do seemingly strange things. But the love of God and the love of neighbor are the motives behind all they do. It was truly love that moved the Curé of Ars to take strong measures to make his flock holy. He realized that there was a judgment hereafter for every pastor of souls.

Lescuyer

Ah!
if we had the eyes of angels with which to see
Our Lord Jesus Christ
Who is here present
on this altar
and Who is looking at us. . . .
how we should love Him!

CHAPTER 9

The Church

IF FATHER VIANNEY realized that the faith of the people of Ars needed to be restored, he realized too that the church of the people of Ars also needed to be restored. A beautiful church can be an actual grace attracting people and warming their hearts. When the Curé first visited the church of St. Sixtus, he found it poor both without and within. The walls were whitewashed, and the flat ceiling was full of cracks. The poverty of the church stirred the compassion of visiting priests. Even the few vestments were poor and threadbare. But the Curé loved his church just the same, and he prayed before the Blessed Sacrament as if he were in a cathedral.

What would the Curé do first to beautify the church? Jesus must have a new setting! Therefore, the Curé ordered a new altar and paid for it himself. Then he walked to Lyons and carried back two statues of angels to set on either side of the tabernacle. But the woodwork seemed faded beside the new altar. So he himself set to work and painted the woodwork with something bright and fresh.

Again the Curé went to Lyons. He hurried

about here and there visiting the workshops of the embroiderers and of the goldsmith, ordering only the most precious vessels and vestments to add to the "household possessions of the good God." His own cassock could be of old rags, but the vestments of God must be of rich silk. As a result, the little church came into the possession of goods of great worth—but not of great artistic value.

In 1820, directions were given to erect a new bell tower for which the Curé bought a second bell that he paid for himself and blessed with the name of the Holy Rosary. Gradually, the side chapels were added: Our Lady's, which was completed for the parish feast on August 6, 1820; St. John the Baptist's, which was opened on the saint's feast, June 24, 1823; St. Philomena's, which was finished in 1837; and finally the chapels of the Ecce Homo and of the Holy Angels. He had also planned a chapel in honor of St. Joseph, but it was never erected. Each Saturday morning for forty years the Curé offered Holy Mass in the chapel of Our Lady.

The chapel of St. John the Baptist was blessed by his classmate, the future bishop of Dubuque, Abbé Mathias Loras. Here the confessional of the Curé stood. Because his Confirmation patron was St. John, the Curé promised to pay for the chapel himself. But when the carpenter wanted his money, the Curé found himself without a single coin. Being anxious about his predicament, he took a quiet walk in order to think, and to receive light and guidance from the Holy Spirit. On the way he met a woman. "Are you the Curé of Ars?" she inquired. He answered that he was. With that she handed him six hundred francs. His problem was solved, but he made a resolution for the future always to pay in advance.

Over the arch of St. John's chapel was written an inscription which all the parishioners well understood: "His head was the price of a dance." One Sunday, when referring to the chapel of St. John, he said to the people: "My brethren, if you knew what had happened in that chapel, you would be afraid to go into it.... I will say no more." Did he receive a vision of the future, of the throngs who would come to that chapel for confession? He merely said, "I will say no more."

Gradually, the little church was filled with all the Curé's close friends, the saints. He used to say, "Sometimes the mere sight of a picture is enough to move and convert us." Here and there in the church and chapels were found, besides Our Lady, St. Joseph and St. Philomena, many others of his heavenly companions: St. Peter, St. Sixtus, St. Blaise, St. John the Baptist, St. Lawrence, St. Francis of Assisi, St. Catherine of Siena, St. Joseph Benedict Labre, and the Archangels Michael and Raphael. We are told that the big statues threw him into raptures. "Ah, if we had faith!" he would sigh.

Where did he get all the money to carry on these improvements? Was not Ars a poor parish? Someone has solved the difficulty by explaining,

"Father Vianney needed but to ask, and he would immediately obtain all that he required for his church." Probably the greatest benefactor of the church was Vicomte Francis, brother of Mlle. des Garets, who ordered from Paris and Lyons box after box of furnishings for the church. "The village sanctuary will never appear so splendid and magnificent as I wish to see it," the Vicomte wrote to his sister. For example, in 1827, the Vicomte sent to Ars a silver-gilt monstrance, a throne for Exposition, a tabernacle of gilt brass, and other elaborate furnishings. How the Curé thrilled whenever a box arrived for the church! When he opened his treasures, he would exclaim, "Ah, in Heaven everything will be even more beautiful!"

On and on went the repairs and improvements for the house of God! The front entrance to the church was widened, and the porch with steps and a graceful railing was added in 1826. This was to be crowned later with a statue of Mary Immaculate. In 1845, the whole sanctuary was lengthened and a second sacristy added. It was at this time that the Curé placed a confessional behind the high altar for the confessions of priests.

In spite of all these improvements—made solely for the honor and glory of God—the original church lost none of its humility and simplicity. The parishioners loved it, and there the visitors found God. And the Curé grew in heroic sanctity before its tabernacle.

CHAPTER 10

Trials

NESTLED in the beautiful green countryside
of the *department* of the Rhone was the tiny
village of Salles. Its people were good, and its
fresh air was just what the Curé of Ars needed
for his health—so thought the chancery officials
in Lyons. Therefore in April, 1820, the Curé
received an appointment to Salles.

It was not long before the mayor of Ars and
a delegation of the people set out for the chancery office in Lyons with a petition: Ars begs to
keep its parish priest. "If that be so," agreed the
kind Vicar General, Father Courbon, "let him
remain as long as he likes." Even the good Lord
agreed with this decision, because the river Saone
was so swollen by the floods that the boatman
was afraid to ferry the Curé with his library and
furniture across the wild, rushing waters. After
two unsuccessful attempts to cross the river, the
Curé with his belongings returned to Ars—for
good.

One year later, on June 20, 1821, Father Courbon made the Curé of Ars a resident pastor. Until
then, the church at Ars had been a kind of mission of the church at Mizerieux, a village about

two miles away. From now on, Ars was to be an independent parish.

Not for long, however, was Ars destined to be parish in the great archdiocese of Lyons. In the southeastern corner of the *department* of Ain is the city of Belley. In 1823, the diocese of Belley was re-established, and Ars, which was located in the Ain, became a part of this diocese. No sooner was the diocese established than Bishop Devie began to receive anonymous letters full of complaints about the Curé of Ars. So many letters came that the Bishop was forced to send to Ars the pastor of Trevoux, Father Vianney's dean, to make a thorough investigation of the many accusations brought against the pastor of Ars.

What was the trouble? Had not the people of Ars begged Father Courbon to return their pastor when he had been appointed to Salles? Did they not love him? The good loved him, and loved him as their father. But there were others who were the object of his vehement sermons against taverns, against dancing, against Sunday work, and against evil of all kinds. They did not love; they sought to get even with him by dishonoring his reputation through anonymous letters sent to the chancery at Belley. "If on my arrival at Ars," the Curé confided many years later, "I had foreseen all that I was to suffer there, I should have died on the spot." Yet, he explained firmly to his people during a Sunday sermon that a pastor who wants to do his duty must keep his sword in hand at all times. Perhaps he had in mind the words of St. Paul: "But I will most gladly spend and be spent myself for your souls even though, loving you more, I be loved less." [*2 Cor.* 12:15].

Those who were opposed to the new regime also instigated a whispering campaign in Ars against the pastor. They tried to start the rumor that his pallor and emaciation were not due to his penances, but due to secret debauchery. His name was woven into their cheap songs. His name was even attached to a wretched girl on the occasion of a village scandal. Anonymous letters of a foul nature were also sent to him, and placards of the same kind were nailed up on the rectory. For a year and a half, a miserable woman used to sneak about the rectory, night after night, and call out loathsome accusations against the pastor.

Things got so bad that the good Curé decided to leave Ars; he would no longer then be the occasion of this disgraceful wrong. But a friend explained to him that by leaving, he would only seem to confirm the evil rumors. So he stayed on. "We must pray for them," he kept repeating to the mayor. "We must pray for them!"

Added to this agony of being the center of an evil campaign was the constant fear the Curé had of losing his own soul. "My God," he used to plead, "make me suffer whatsoever You wish to inflict on me, but grant that I may not fall into Hell." Thus he suffered on and on until God relieved him by sending him the special grace of finding perfect joy in carrying the cross. A time was to come when he would be able to say with certain conviction: "To suffer lovingly is to suffer no longer. To flee from the cross is to be crushed beneath its weight. We should pray for a love of the cross—then it will become sweet."

The dean could find nothing wrong with the Curé on the occasion of his investigation. Was not the Curé's reserve in his relationship with women to be commended? It was said that he would not even pat the head of a little girl. One witness reported that he was so scrupulous in this matter that he rebuked some little girls who had presumed merely to touch the hand of a passing ecclesiastic. When in the presence of women, the Curé always stood, spoke briefly, kept perfect modesty of his eyes, and never partook of frivolity; he kept his manner serious and grave. Catherine Lassagne, who helped him in the parish in many wonderful ways and who served him solely for the love of God, revealed in later years: "Whenever I brought him anything I was always prepared to be sent away." When the Curé abolished the office of housekeeper, he permitted a very devout woman to come once in a while to clean the rectory a bit—but she was to come only when he was out. So spotless and prudent were the life and habits of the Curé of Ars that the investigation of the Bishop was dropped.

The Curé of Ars was now over forty and growing old fast. He was not well and was ailing from fever and from many physical disorders. In the summer of 1827 he consented to see a doctor. Fearing that his condition might become chronic, the doctor prescribed a more nourishing diet of milk, soups, chicken, beer, toast with fresh butter, tea with milk and sugar, and other substantial foods. The Curé thanked the doctor, got a packet of tea, and went back to the rectory. That was the last that we hear of this special diet.

The fever never left the Curé, and being weary both in body and in mind, he himself finally asked for a change to another parish. The Bishop was most considerate and offered him the parish of Fareins. This parish was about five times the size of Ars and truly a mission parish where the apostolic zeal of the Curé could do much good. The Curé analyzed the change prayerfully, and eventually confided to one of his friends: "Unhappy man that I am! Here am I prepared to take charge of a large parish when I am hard put to it not to give way to despair in a small one."

Father Vianney stayed on at Ars. God wanted him just where he was. His body grew thin, his fever grew worse, and his discipline found no rest. But the conversion of Ars—and the conversion of many souls in France—was about to blossom forth.

CHAPTER 11

Transformation

MOST OF THE trials that Father Vianney had to endure during the early years of his pastorate were caused by a few whom ignorance and sin had confused. Jesus Himself had His enemies; and he who tried so earnestly to walk in the footsteps of Jesus could not expect to walk in those footsteps without enemies trailing him in his pathway. As late as 1830, an occasional ember of resentment on the part of some families was still smoldering. This hurt the Curé, especially when the resentment burst forth again into flame, and seven parishioners petitioned him to *get out* of the parish. The petition failed; and as a whole, the parish at Ars was gradually dawning into a new day. Peace, which only God can give, was beginning to spread its radiance throughout the village and the surrounding countryside. "Ah, my brethren," the good Curé exclaimed in 1827 at one of his instructions, "Ars is Ars no longer! I have heard confessions and preached at jubilees and missions, but never have I found anything to compare with what I witness here."

Many careless people were becoming good; good people were growing better; and the better people were practicing the heroism of saints. Girls and women joined the Guild of the Holy Rosary; boys and men became members of the Guild of the Blessed Sacrament which the Curé had revived. However, the boys and men never attained the great spirituality that the Curé had set for them. It was difficult to free them entirely from the slavery of human respect.

The great personal devotion of the Curé himself was his devotion to Jesus in the Blessed Sacrament. He knew that love for the Blessed Sacrament was the most powerful means of renewing the heart of a parish. He inspired his people, mostly by personal example, often to make visits. The school teacher, Mr. Pertinand, testified, "I cannot recollect a single occasion when, on entering the church, I did not find someone or other in adoration." Such was the devotion to the Blessed Sacrament by 1825. Even some men left their farm tools leaning against the wall of the church while they made a visit. One of the men, Mr. Chaffangeon—a dear old man who did not know many prayers—told the Curé one day, "I look at the good God, and He looks at me." His was a simple faith in the Blessed Sacrament like the simple faith of an adoring angel. Perhaps fifty women and maybe a dozen men attended daily Mass. Some families tried to have a representative at Holy Mass each day. Holy Communion, especially frequent Holy Communion, was encouraged in many inventive ways: the people were urged to receive on anniversaries, on the occasion of a

Baptism, or a marriage, or on any big feast or holiday.

The climax of the Curé's ardent love for the Eucharist came on Corpus Christi. On that feast, he was all smiles. He had already encouraged as many homes as possible to build altars of repose so that the parish would be blessed by a multiplicity of Benedictions. There were altar boys, flower girls, and a huge procession of all the people, for he would tolerate no spectators. Never did he weary of carrying the heavy monstrance. "Why should I be tired?" he questioned a sympathizer. "He whom I carried likewise carried me." The only joy that could approach that of Corpus Christi was the joy of Holy Thursday, when he used to remain all night on his knees in silent adoration.

Truly Ars was Ars no longer! When the Curé came to the village, the Rosary was recited publicly only once a year, on the Annunciation. But it was not long before the evening bell summoned the villagers to the church where their pastor led them, night after night, in the recitation of the Rosary and night prayers. Those who could not come prayed at home; the men coming in from the fields at least fingered their rosaries as they walked beside their carts.

Gradually the habit of asking the blessing before meals and of giving the thanksgiving after meals became the common thing to do. Whenever the Angelus bell rang, the people honored Our Lady with their Aves without any notice of human respect, even though the ringing of the bell found them laboring out in the fields. Some followed the example of the Curé and blessed the hour with a Hail Mary when the church clock struck the hour. In this atmosphere of prayer, the habit of swearing ceased altogether. As one peasant remarked, "It would be too shameful a thing to commit such sins when we live close to a saint."

Sometimes the neighboring villagers would sneer, "If you listen to your pastor, he will turn you all into Capuchins." But the faithful souls only answered, "Our Curé is a saint; we must obey him." At Ars, the good Curé began to be loved as a father, and obeyed as a king. The time was to come soon when no one would dare speak but well of the Curé of Ars.

The faith was so weak in many neighboring villages (because of the lack of priests and because of the Revolution) that many of the pastors invited the Curé of Ars to come and preach at their missions or at their forty hours devotions, and help arouse the faith of their people. The Curé was always willing to help a fellow priest. Perhaps he was even exploited. At Limas, where he was invited to preach, the Curé was unnerved when he found the sanctuary full of priests waiting to hear his sermon. "However," he said later, "I began to speak of the love of God, and apparently all went well: everybody wept." While attending these missions, he spent most of his time in the confessional. At the rectory, he maintained his usual simple diet. However, at Montmerle he roomed at the house of a parishioner, and during his stay his only food was a saucepan of potatoes. "I have a good workman," said the pastor of Montmerle concerning the pastor of Ars. "He works hard and eats nothing."

He walked back and forth from Ars to the various missions, tramping along, fingering his rosary, stopping to visit the sick when he reached the boundaries of his parish, or recounting an interesting story from the life of some saint if perchance he picked up with a fellow traveler. Once his companion, Anthony Mandy, the young son of the mayor, complained about the cold. "My friend," the Curé counseled kindly, "the saints have suffered far more; let us offer it all to the good God."

Gradually the seeds of conversion in the village of Ars were beginning to brighten into reality. The whole parish was solidly forming into a living shrine. But the work of the Curé was not to end with Ars and its neighboring villages. There was still the work of the conversion of thousands of souls who would make their way in pilgrimage to this shrine of Ars to experience its peace and to meet its living flame—the holy Curé himself.

Lescuyer

What happiness do we not feel
in the Presence of God
when we feel ourselves alone
at His feet
before the Holy tabernacle!

CHAPTER 12

Providence

ON JULY 8, 1819, the father of the Curé of Ars died, and his name was reverently placed in the memento of every Mass offered by his devoted son. The Curé received a small legacy from his father, which he invested in a fund for the foundation of a girls' school. He who suffered much from a lack of education set out to remedy such a lack in others—at least in the girls of the village. A school for the boys would come later. In the meantime, the boys would have to shift for themselves. Ars at that time possessed no school of any kind worthy of the name.

For teachers in his proposed school, the Curé selected two good, simple young women, Catherine Lassagne and Benoite Lardet, whom he sent to study with the Sisters of St. Joseph at Fareins. Meanwhile, he drained his resources by purchasing a newly erected three-room house near the church as his new school. In November, 1824, the free school was opened with his two teachers in charge. Jeanne-Marie Chanay also offered her services as cook, baker, laundress—and *human-cross* for Catherine. Marie Filliat later joined the staff after the beautiful death of Catherine's

friend, Benoite, in 1830. No salary was given to
the young teachers. Their only reward was the
satisfaction of realizing that they were serving God
under the direction of a saint. They lived in
poverty and in trust that God would provide.
Fittingly, therefore, the school was called "Providence."

Since it was a free school, girls came even from
neighboring villages. With the attic as a dormi-
tory, the small house became a boarding school;
during the first year, there were sixteen boarders.
The children came with sheets and blankets, and
God's Providence provided for everything else.
There were also in the neighborhood orphans and
poor little illegitimate girls thrown out upon the
mercy of the world. These unfortunate ones, the
charity of the Curé embraced also. By 1827 these
were the only girls admitted as boarders; girls from
the better homes were received as day students.
All the boarders were called orphans, and they
ranged in age from eight to twenty: poor, un-
derfed, unwanted, half clad. They were all huddled together into the three rooms and the attic
of Providence—but somehow, there was always
a place for one more.

"Receive this child whom the good God sends
to you," the Curé pleaded one day to Catherine
as he brought in a girl whom he had found wandering about the village."

"But, Father, there is no vacant bed."

"There is always yours," smiled the Curé and
left the child with Catherine.

The Curé's one ambition was to make of these girls good Catholics, good mothers, and even, he hoped, good religious—but his ambition caused him many anxious moments. The cash box was too often empty. It was hard enough for the parishioners to give up taverns and dances, without expecting them to sacrifice for charity, too. Every now and then the Curé used to set out for the homes of charitable Catholics in Lyons as "a traveler in behalf of Providence," as he was wont to call himself jokingly. Providence always provided!

Like the mother hen, Catherine never counted the girls and never kept statistics. She did not have time. For years, the house was always full, squeezing as many as sixty into those small rooms. "This was no ordinary institution," wrote a lawyer of Lyons. "It was truly the product of the holiness of its founder. The temporal resources, the life, spirit, and guidance of the home came from him."

The children were often in want. But Providence always provided. In 1829 they had no corn. The Curé casually buried his relic of St. Francis Regis in the tiny pile of corn they had scraped together, and prayed. Later, Jeanne-Marie, the cook, seeking the corn that was left, went up into the attic of the rectory where it was stored. No sooner had she tried the door than she screamed down to the Curé, "Your attic is full!"

At another time, out of scarcely enough flour for three loaves of bread, miraculously ten large loaves were baked. Of this the Curé simply remarked: "The good God is very good! He takes care of His poor."

Without question, the school was the one undertaking which brought the Curé the greatest consolation. "Only on the day of Judgment will men see how much good has been accomplished in that institution," he used to say. From 1827 he took his meals at the school, his cup of milk or his crust of bread. For this, five minutes were sufficient. With this system, he was freed of the bother of being his own cook.

The simple lessons in reading and writing, knitting and sewing, were closed each morning with the recitation of the litany of Divine Providence. Following the litany, the door softly opened and in walked the good pastor for his daily catechism lesson. Everything was simple: his language, his examples, his explanations. Sometimes parishioners joined the class; in time pilgrims joined. The room was so small that the people stood outside and listened through the open windows. By 1845 the lessons proved to be so very popular that the daily catechism instruction had to be given over in the church in order to accommodate the crowds. It was better then: the Curé was closer to his Eucharistic King.

The Curé wanted to establish perpetual adoration in the Providence by building a side chapel, there to retire and be with God. He built the side chapel, but to retire was not among God's plans for him.

As time went on, the Bishop feared that when the Curé should go, the school and orphanage would go too. He believed that the orphanage should be abandoned for the present and that the school should be placed in the hands of a sisterhood. (The Curé did not live to see the reopening of his orphanage in 1863). This truly crushed the Curé. They were taking from him his one attachment, if such it could be called. He said nothing—it was God's will—but he was cut deeply. Catherine likewise was broken in spirit, but she was encouraged to see in it all the way of Divine Providence.

Negotiations were carried on; a deed was drawn up, signed, and sealed; and on November 5, 1848, the Sisters of St. Joseph took possession of the little school. There were no hard feelings, but the *human* suffered much. Catherine Lassagne and Marie Filliat settled down in two small rooms near the rectory and cared for the linens and decorated the altars in the church. The Curé went back to the rectory for his meals, but did not abandon the children and the Sisters. He was good to the Sisters; in fact, through his own intervention, one of his nieces became a Sister of St. Joseph. After officiating at the renewing of the Sisters' vows in the new chapel of the Providence, July 2, 1855, the Curé could not restrain his overflowing happiness. "Oh, how beautiful is religion!" he exclaimed. "I was thinking a little while ago that between Our Lord and these good religious, His mystic brides, there took place a contest in generosity. But, do what they may, Our Lord invariably proves the winner. The Sisters said: 'I renew my vows of poverty, chastity, and obedience.' Yet it was they who received most, for I in my turn said: 'May the Body of Our Lord Jesus Christ keep thy soul unto life everlasting.' ''

His Providence was gone; it was no longer his own. The Curé continued to do his duty, but his heart was no longer in the work. He never failed to bless the little girls and encourage them to be good, but his heart he placed in another field of labor for souls. They had taken his Providence, but he still clung to his altar, his pulpit, and his confessional.

The good Curé did not forget his boys all the while he was working for his girls. He himself paid for the school fees of poor boys, and often visited the classroom of Jean Pertinard, the village schoolmaster, who was the nephew of a priest and an excellent Catholic. In fact, the Curé was the one who prevailed upon the mayor to hire this fine man for the post of teacher, which he held from 1835 until 1849.

The Curé's dream of a Catholic school for boys was realized on March 10, 1849 when three Brothers of the Holy Family of Belley came to Ars to continue the work of Jean Pertinard. The superior was a young religious of twenty-four, Brother Athanase, who was destined to conduct the school at Ars for forty-one years. He was to become a very important part of the village: he played the organ, taught plainchant, trained the altar boys, and became a kind of historian of the holy Curé of Ars. "Open a boarding school," the Curé told the superior. "You will succeed. You will see that you will snatch many youthful souls from the devil."

In the same year that the new school for boys was opened, the Curé of Ars began another wonderful educational program: the establishment of missions to be held periodically in the churches of neighboring villages. "I love the missions to such an extent," he exclaimed one day from the pulpit, "that if, by selling my body, I could establish another, I should sell it." At the time of his death, the mission-minded Curé had provided in various poor parishes for close to one hundred missions to be repeated at intervals of ten years.

He who suffered so much in being without education, suffered much too in trying to promote education. But the Curé's labors for girls and boys and souls continued and prospered for his greater glory even after his soul had long since left his beloved village of Ars.

CHAPTER 13

Pilgrimage

IN ALL of God's kingdom, nothing on earth attracts more than heroic holiness in action— especially in modern days. Seldom does a man living today become a walking relic, a human shrine, or the object of pilgrimage for a span of over thirty years. From 1827 until 1859, the church at Ars was never empty. People streamed to see its Curé. At first, in 1827, about twenty visitors a day came to the village; then as time went on, the twenty swelled into crowds, until Ars became the focal center of spirituality in France.

How did this happen? In the early years at Ars, people from Dardilly, his home town, and from Ecully where he served as assistant, visited the Curé. Others came from Les Robins—the young man whom they admired as a fugitive, they now wished to consult as a priest. As early as 1822, the simple and devout spoke of him as the *holy* Curé of Ars. Those who had heard him preach at missions and at Forty Hours devotions in the neighboring villages and who had received his counsel in the confessional, hungered for more of his preaching and counsel; so they came to Ars. Also, the story of the multiplication of the corn and the loaves of bread had spread around the countryside. Using the assumption that if two miracles are possible, more miracles are probable, the sick and the infirm hobbled into Ars hoping and praying for a cure.

Undoubtedly, human nature being what it is, curiosity was one of the chief attractions to Ars. People had heard that a real, living saint dwelt in France. Who does not want to see a saint—not a dead one, but a talking one? So the curious came to Ars—but more often than not, they returned to their homes, cured of the curiosity and confessed of their sins. The name of the Curé was on the lips of everyone; they could utter nothing but, "He is not like other men!"

Because of the possibility of deception, and because of the incalculable danger that can follow upon error in the hearts of the faithful, the Church and churchmen have always been reluctant to accept the extraordinary readily. Hence, not infrequently, the greatest opposition in the beginning to the Church's mystics has been from the Church herself. Many sad instances in her history have taught her the wisdom of this procedure. It is no wonder then that his fellow priests were slow to *accept* the heroism of the Curé of Ars. Priests are usually the last to be convinced; they trust a dead saint more than a living saint.

The Curé was greatly criticized. His colleagues remembered well his lack of education. Is he not the lad whom Father Balley pushed through the seminary? Who does he think that he is, getting all those people to crowd around him? After all, he is only the pastor of Ars—what can be worse? Why does he not act more like the other priests in the neighborhood? Why, once he sat next to the Bishop, and did not even wear a sash. At clerical conferences, he always looks poor and contemptible. At least he can buy a few new clothes; he cannot be that poor. Maybe he is just hoarding his money. There are symptoms of hypocrisy about him. Even some of his judgments seem faulty and strange. All this can be a trick to attract attention—a Pharisaical trumpet-blowing. Still people are naive enough to consult him. In fact, pilgrimages are being formed to Ars. There is talk of miracles. Scandalous! The Bishop ought to know about this. Maybe the wise old Curé has already got him under his spell. At any rate, my people will be forbidden to go there under pain of refusal of absolution. The scandal of Ars must be proclaimed from our pulpits.

"Poor little Curé of Ars!" groaned the Curé himself when he heard all the talk that was flooding the area. "What do they not make him say; what do they not make him do! At present, it is on him they preach, and no longer on the Gospel!" To one of his fellow priests who, in fraternal charity, offered the much-maligned Pastor of Ars counsel, the Curé wrote: "I thank you most sincerely for the kind advice which you have the charity to give me. I acknowledge my ignorance and my incapacity. Pray to God, Father, that I may do less harm and more good." When some of the priests finally sent a letter of denunciation to the Bishop, the humble Curé countersigned the letter himself, remarking, "Now they have my signature, so there will be no lack of material to lead to a conviction."

Bishop Devie was a wise and prudent man—a holy Bishop. Before acting, he sent to Ars his austere Vicar General, Father Ruivet, to secure the fullest possible information. The Vicar General lived with the Curé, talked with him, questioned him. He concluded, "If the denunciations were based on facts, we should not see so many pilgrims here, and among them both religious and priests." The Bishop was satisfied. Yet, to be absolutely certain, he requested the Curé of Ars to forward his most difficult cases to him, together with the solution he had suggested for each. Within a few years, the Curé had sent in more than two hundred cases, all of which, after close examination, were found to be extremely prudent. Later, when the Bishop overheard some of his clergy referring to the *madness* of the Curé of Ars, he remarked, "Gentlemen, I could wish that all my clergy had a small grain of the same madness."

By 1834 matters began to simmer down, and the real sanctity of the Curé of Ars began to impress even his fellow priests. At the priests' retreat of that year in the major seminary at Bourg, the Bishop listed the Curé of Ars as one of the retreat confessors. His confessional was kept so busy by priest-penitents that the Curé had no time to make his own retreat—his life was a perpetual retreat.

Throughout all these periods of storm and stress, the Curé reacted much like the saint in the story he was so fond of telling:

"A certain saint once commanded one of his religious, 'Go into the cemetery and speak as much evil of the dead as you can.' The religious obeyed. On his return the saint asked him, 'What did they answer?' 'Nothing.' 'Well, go back now and pay them a great many compliments.' The religious obeyed once more and returned to his superior. 'Surely this time they said something by way of reply?' 'Again nothing.' 'Very well,' said the saint, 'if people rebuke you, if they praise you, do as the dead.'"

CHAPTER 14

Saint Philomena

SAINTS ARE ingenious in devising ways of preserving their humility. The Curé of Ars was no exception. He openly refused to become the center of attention for the wonders of body and soul that were taking place at Ars. His humility rebelled against the thought of receiving credit. God, in His mercy, came to the Curé's rescue by sending him the relics of St. Philomena, whom the Curé "blamed" for whatever blessings came to Ars. Just when his devotion to St. Philomena became so strong is not known, but once the saint was established at Ars, to her was given the credit for all the wonders that made Ars the great center of pilgrimage.

"The love of the Curé of Ars," writes Father Monnin, "for his 'dear little saint,' as he called her, was almost chivalrous. There was the most touching sympathy between them. She granted everything to his prayers; he refused nothing to her love. He set down to her account all the graces and wonders which contributed to the celebrity of the pilgrimage of Ars. It was all her work; he had nothing whatever to do with it."

In the first or second century of the Church,

a girl of about fourteen years bravely went to her death solely for the love of Jesus. Perhaps, like St. Sebastian, her body was pierced with arrows. However, after her death, she was lovingly buried in the catacomb of St. Priscilla, and three tiles closed her shelf tomb and carried the simple inscription: "Philomena, peace be with you." And thus was a virgin martyr buried and forgotten over the centuries.

On May 24, 1802, Philomena was born anew when her tomb (or cavity) was discovered by some workmen busy clearing out a section of the catacomb. Her skull had been fractured and her phial of blood, symbol of martyrdom, shattered. Workmen gathered her remains into a silk-lined box and carried them to the "Custodia Generale" where precious relics were reserved.

In 1805 Don Francesco, the parish priest of Mugnano near Naples, came to Rome seeking the relics of some martyr to counteract the evils of his parish. Admitted to the Custodia Generale, he soon chose the relics of Philomena. But such a treasure was considered too great for the village of Mugnano. He begged and pleaded; he was again refused. He fell ill, and then beseeched Philomena to cure him and to prove that it was God's will that her relics go back with him to Mugnano. This she did. Thus did the little saint travel back to Mugnano, where her casket was publicly enshrined in the Church of Our Lady of Grace. And immediately the virgin martyr began her work: a bedridden man rose from his cot; a crippled child walked; a blind baby saw; a skeptic believed, and others believed, and soon many believed, and before long devotion to Philomena spread from Mugnano throughout Italy and even up into France.

Father de Mongallon, the superior of the Brothers of St. John of God and a great lover of Philomena, brought the story of the virgin martyr to the Jaricot family in Lyons. Often, he used to stay with this charitable family, and during one of his visits Pauline, when a girl of about seventeen, begged him for a relic. No doubt it was this young martyr who gave Pauline the courage to carry out her program for the Propagation of the Faith. After Philomena was instrumental in curing Pauline of a fatal illness, and after Pauline had come laughing and happy to Pope Gregory XVI with her miraculous story, the Holy Father immediately introduced the cause for the canonization of the virgin martyr.

During one of his visits to the Jaricot family, perhaps when he was begging for his Providence, the Curé of Ars asked Pauline for a small piece from her relic of Philomena. In this simple way, the saint was taken to Ars, where she was destined to be the *sole cause* for all the wonders of that holy place.

However, the people never quite gave all credit to St. Philomena. They believed that she helped, and helped in a marvelous way, but only when her prayers were mingled with those of the Curé. But the Curé insisted: "I do not work miracles.

I am but a poor ignorant man who once upon a time tended sheep. Address yourselves to St. Philomena; I have never asked anything through her without being answered."

When pilgrims would come to him, he would say to them, "Go talk about all this to St. Philomena!" Or he would say, "Have confidence in St. Philomena." Or again he would insist, "Go and ask for your cure in the chapel of St. Philomena; I will pray for you in the meantime." Sometimes he rebuked the young saint for working so many miracles at Ars: "St. Philomena has broken her word," he scolded one day. "She should have cured the child elsewhere!"

The two saints worked on together for the glory of God, and Father Vianney's humility grew stronger and deeper as he continued to point out the way, "Go to Philomena!"

CHAPTER 15

Confessor

DURING the last year of Father Vianney's life, it was estimated that the number of pilgrims to Ars reached between one hundred thousand and one hundred and twenty thousand. In Lyons, there was a special booking office for Ars: in 1840, one train ran daily between Lyons and Ars; by 1855, two trains ran daily. People of all kinds visited the village: those with faith and those who boasted to be without faith; sightseers and the curious; bishops, priests, and religious; good people and bad people; the young and the old— they came to see, to hear, and some to touch the *living* saint of France. However, most of the people came to go to confession or to fulfill a promise made to St. Philomena or to question the good Curé on some problem. Some stayed in one of the five places honored by the title of *hotel;* others remained in the houses of the villagers. During the summer, pilgrims even spent the night sleeping out in the meadows, or resting on the steps of the church. While waiting for the Curé, the pilgrims roamed the streets, talking about the holy priest and buying his picture in souvenir shops. Finding his picture in the stores and houses of

the village bothered the Curé. He hated the idea
of publicity and commercialism. But there was
little he could do about it—except refuse to pose
for his portrait. The pilgrims also purchased
rosaries and medals to be blessed, and candles
to be burned at the shrine of St. Philomena. They
prayed, listened to the catechism lessons, and
above all, waited in line to go to confession.

Waiting in line to go to confession was the trial
and cross of Ars. The Curé spent as much as sixteen to eighteen hours a day in the confessional,
and still there were lines of pilgrims. If a penitent left the line to have lunch, he made arrange-
ments with those next to him or with a church
guardian to save his place. Some penitents brought
lunch with them. At night, before the church was
locked, penitents numbered themselves and re-
sumed the same order in line the next morning.
As many as eighty spent the night outside the
church doors in order to resume the same line
next day. The Curé once admonished an impa-
tient young woman: "You are not very patient,
my child. You have been here only three days and
you want to go home? You must remain fifteen
days. Go and pray to St. Philomena to tell you
what is your vocation, and after that come and
see me." This she did. Later, she became a Sister.

The Curé of Ars usually showed no partiality
save to his parishioners, the sick, and the crippled. Bishops were seen standing in line. However, he seemed to have a keen intuition from the
Holy Spirit that enabled him to pick out souls

who needed God's special grace just at a special moment. "You, madame, are in a hurry. Come at once!" This he said to a mother of sixteen children who was waiting anxiously in line. "You, madame, follow me!" This he said to a woman he met on the street while he was returning from a sick call. It meant her conversion. A sportsman who came to Ars only to satisfy his curiosity and then to go duck hunting happened to meet the Curé crossing the village square. The Curé stopped, looked at the dog and then at the man, and said gravely to the stranger, "Sir, it is greatly to be wished that your soul were as beautiful as your dog!" The Curé went on; the sportsman blushed. Something pierced his soul! He rushed his way through the crowds, ran to confession only to hear three words, "Go to La Trappe!" This he did and was professed Brother Arsene.

The words of the Curé were darts; they penetrated deeply. He said little. But his little was enough. To this one or to that one he would simply say:

"You have a vice that will be your damnation— namely, pride!" This to a woman.

"My friend, you are damned!" This he said to a young man who later repented.

"Love your priests much!" This to a bishop.

"Oh! love, love the good God very much!" This he said to a Brother.

"What a pity!" That was all he said—but it was enough for many penitents.

Many came to the Curé seeking advice on a

religious vocation. Often he would lift his eyes to Heaven and then give a decision, not only without hesitation but also with much certainty, as if he actually heard the Holy Spirit:

"Enter at once the Visitation," he counseled a girl.

"Stay where you are," he recommended to a priest who wished to enter a religious order. "You see, the good God at times inspires us with desires of which He will never ask the fulfillment in this world."

"Be sure you do no such a thing," the Curé replied to a colonel in uniform who wished to become a religious. "The army has too great a need of an example such as you give."

To a priest engaged in teaching at a Catholic college Father Vianney insisted: "Be sure you never become a pastor. The most beautiful task anyone can perform in the century in which we live is the Christian education of youth."

To another priest who complained about the indifference of the people in his parish, the Curé answered: "You have preached; you have prayed. But have you fasted? Have you taken the discipline? Have you slept on the bare floor? So long as you have done none of these things, you have no right to complain."

Then added to the burning words of the Curé—few though they were—were his tears. Tears are the outward expression of sincerity. Those tears of the Curé uttered messages of which mere words are entirely barren. "Why do you weep so much, Father?" "Ah, my friend," sighed the Curé to a sinner kneeling beside him, "I weep because you do not weep enough!" His tears which flowed so naturally down furrows that were grooved deeply over the years were the most irrestistible characteristic of the Curé. He wept over poor sinners. His poor sinners! "If only I could go to confession for them," he used to grieve. And again, he would remark with tears in his eyes, "I am only content when praying for sinners."

Did the Curé give big penances to big sinners? At first, perhaps he did. It was the spirit of the times. But later, through reading, advice, and experience, he changed. He believed that people who came far, and who endured many sacrifices, would become discouraged with big penances. To a fellow priest, he once remarked, "My friend, here is my recipe: I give them a small penance and the remainder I myself perform in their stead."

To those good souls who wished to advance in the way of perfection, he advised the practice of daily meditation, and taught them how to make it. For spiritual reading he recommended the Gospels, the *Imitation of Christ*, and the Lives of the Saints.

To a mother of a large family who was expecting another child, he said with fatherly kindness and consideration: "Be comforted, my child. If you only knew the women who will go to Hell because they did not bring into the world the children they should have given to it!"

Gradually the years of labor in God's vineyard

bent the shoulders of the Curé and turned his flowing hair to white. But he himself remarked in his own poetic way, "In a soul united to God, it is always springtime."

CHAPTER 16

The Devil

EVEN THE DEVIL came to Ars. Indeed, he had a reason. By the mouth of a possessed woman, he exclaimed one day to the Curé, "How thou makest me suffer! If there were three men on earth like thyself, my kingdom would be destroyed." Father Vianney was outwitting the proud devil by saving so many souls. The kingdom of Heaven seemed to be growing faster than the kingdom of Hell. Frustrated, the devil would roar like a bull, growl like a bear, or snarl like a dog in an effort to intimidate the Curé. With a fearful voice he would cry out: "Vianney! Vianney! Potato eater! Ah, thou art not yet dead! I shall get thee, all right."

"The devil," according to Father Tanquerey, "jealous of God's influence on the souls of the Saints, strives to exercise his own dominion, or rather his tyranny, over men. At times he, so to speak, besieges the soul from without by assailing it with horrible temptations. (This is called obsession.) The devil can act upon all the external senses: upon the sense of hearing, by causing blasphemous or obscene words or songs to be heard or by creating frightful noises, such as were experienced at times by the sainted Curé of Ars." (*The Spiritual Life*, The Very Rev. Adolphe Tan- querey, p. 718.)

For about thirty-five years (1824-1858), the devil tried in vain to discourage the Curé in his work for souls. But the devil fought a losing battle. As the wind fans the flame to burn more brightly, so those diabolical manifestations, far from snuff- ing out the Curé's efforts for souls, served rather to enkindle his zeal.

At first, the Curé thought a swarm of rats and mice had invaded his rectory. So he placed a pitch- fork near the head of his bed. Night would come—and with the night, noises. It seemed as if the rodents tore the curtains of his bed to threads. But when morning came, he would find all the curtains intact. Soon the Curé feared to remain alone at night. He invited a husky young man of the village, Andrew Verchére, to stay at the rectory with him. He lasted only one night. At one o'clock, the handle and lock of the front door were violently shaken. Then the blows, like those of a club, pounded against the door. At the same time, the racket of the rumbling of many carts seemed to fill the rectory. "My poor Verchére," the Curé told later, "was shaking with fear. Though he was holding his gun in his hand, he no longer knew he had a gun."

It was not long before the Curé realized the true nature of the uproar. "I came to the conclu- sion," he admitted to the Bishop, "that it was the devil, because I was afraid. The good God does

not frighten us." When he had reached that con-
clusion the Curé dismissed his bodyguard, dis-
carded his pitchfork, and girded himself to meet
the devil alone—ready (strong in faith) to resist
the adversary. His weapons were many relics in-
cased in a large silver reliquary, prayer, the Sign
of the Cross, and words of contempt and scorn
for the devil. To belittle the whole situation, he
nicknamed the devil the "grappin." His simple remark to those who questioned him was, "One
gets used to everything, my friend. The *grappin*
and I are almost comrades."

The *grappin* had work to do, and he did it.
Nightly, he visited the Curé, annoying him by
his continual and never-ending noise. Noise, noise,
noise—that was his secret weapon. He reproduced
the sound of a hammer driving nails into a
wooden floor; he drummed on the table; he
screeched a shrill song. "The *grappin* has a very
ugly voice indeed," dryly quipped the Curé. At
times the Curé would feel a hand passing over
his face, or a drove of rats running over his body.
Now he would be jerked from his bed; then again
he would feel as if his hard bed were soft, sensu-
ous and tempting. The whole rectory seemed as
infested with the devil's presence as with the darkness of the night. Once the evil spirit tried to
set fire to his bed. The Curé simply remembered,
"The villainous *grappin!* He could not catch the
bird, so he burns the cage."

Some of his fellow priests insinuated that all
this was probably a figment of the Curé's

imagination. "It is your head," some of them remarked, "that plays you tricks!" However, in a short time they changed their minds. A jubilee was being preached in a neighboring church, and the Curé of Ars was invited. Because of the distance, many of the priests remained for the night, including Father Vianney. After all had retired, the stillness of the night was suddenly broken by a sound like the rumbling of a heavy cart. The rectory shook. An uproar arose in Father Vianney's room. "The Curé of Ars is being murdered!" The priests rushed to his room, threw open the door, burst into the room—only to find the good Curé resting peacefully on his bed. "It is the *grappin*," he said with a smile. "I am sorry I forgot to warn you beforehand. However, it is a good sign: there will be a big fish tomorrow." There was. And the priests believed.

Soon, the *grappin* became a kind of messenger of big sinners. When the devil suspected ahead of time that a big sinner was returning to confession, in his jealousy, he would take out his vengeance on the Curé of Ars. Once after a night of hellish hubbub, the Curé mentioned to a villager, "No doubt at this very moment there are some sinners on the road to Ars."

The devil could not win; and coward that he is, gradually he gave up his nightly visits. Hell was more pleasant than defeat; fire burns less than broken pride. So the devil returned to Hell, and the Curé went on saving souls in Ars.

Lescuyer

How pleasing to Him is the short quarter of an hour
that we steal from our occupations
from something of no use
to come and pray to Him
to visit Him
to console Him
for all the outrages He receives!

CHAPTER 17

Flight

GOD GAVE THE Curé of Ars the soul of a contemplative; yet He destined him to live a life of endless, apostolic activity—his cross! "Since the age of eleven," he once admitted to the mayor, "I have been asking God to let me live in solitude; my prayers have never been answered." At another time, he revealed to a friend, "The good God grants me nearly all that I ask, except when I pray for myself."

That native, inner drive for solitude was intensified all the more by the well-nigh obsession that he had been guilty of presumption in assuming the responsibilities of a parish. "Ah!" he used to sigh deeply, "it is not the labor that costs. That which terrifies me is the account that I must give as Curé...You do not know what it is to pass from the care of souls to the tribunal of God." One day in his catechism class, the Curé fearfully remarked, "Oh! had I known what it means to be a priest, I would promptly have taken refuge at La Trappe." That was the little corner he often referred to when he sought "a little corner where he might weep over his poor life"—La Trappe or La Chartreuse.

It could be, too, that these drives for solitude were only strong temptations of the devil. His kingdom again was threatened as in the days of Christ. As then, so now—he wished to destroy the work of the Curé by suggesting what appeared to be a greater good. Years later, a fellow priest wrote to the Curé cautioning that his longing for solitude was a temptation of the devil. The letter made a lasting impression; it brought to mind the warning of Christ about the wolves in sheep's clothing.

Probably God was only perfecting His servant by the martyrdom of obedience. To remain in the active apostolate in obedience to his Bishop was truly a martyrdom for the contemplative soul of the Curé of Ars.

On numerous occasions, he petitioned his Bishop to grant him a change, or to permit him to say farewell forever to the active life. He longed to have the Bishop visit Ars, for it gave him another chance to make his petition in person. "The Bishop is coming, and I am going to ask him—you know what." But the Bishop's answer was always the same. On three separate occasions, the Curé tried to run away from his parish.

The first attempt was in 1840. Few knew of it. About two in the morning, the Curé left the rectory and took to the road. He was headed for Villefranche, when the inspiration struck him: "Is not the conversion of even one soul of greater value than all the prayers that I might say in solitude?" The inspiration fell on good soil. The Curé immediately returned to Ars.

The second attempt was more involved. On the evening of May 3, 1843, the Curé fell dangerously sick while reciting the May devotions to Our Lady. Everyone believed his end had come. Days passed, and recovery seemed far from near. The Curé himself longed to live longer "in order to weep for my sins and to do a little good." Four doctors were present for consultation; seven priests were at hand for the anointing. The Curé thought that most of the devils of Hell were infesting his room to snatch his soul. They seemed to rasp, "We have him! We have him! He is ours!"

On May 11, one of the doctors whispered, "He has only thirty or forty minutes to live." The Curé overheard him and thought, "My God, I shall then have to appear before Thee empty-handed!" Trustingly he turned to Our Lady and his little Philomena, and they turned to him. The dawn of May 12 found the Curé still breathing; on May 20, the Curé was offering a Mass at the altar of Our Lady in thanksgiving. The doctors described his cure as marvelous. "Miraculous," was the rejoinder of the Curé.

The Curé honestly believed that he had been cured, not for the care of other souls, but for the care of his own soul. He spent that summer regaining his strength by eating *two* meals a day—one with meat! "I have become a glutton," he complained. By September 11, his strength was such that he could flee during the night from his parish of Ars towards his brother's home at

Dardilly. He had written his plan to the Bishop—
and intended to await the answer at Dardilly. In
the interim, he had asked Father Raymond of
Savigneux to *cover* for him. After ten Rosaries
and seven hours, the Curé was back in his old
homestead and Ars was without its beloved Curé.

The Curé was blessed with a little rest, and
then things began to happen. The mayor came
to Dardilly; letters came; on Friday, pilgrims
came; and on Saturday, more pilgrims: Francis
Pertinard and a group of twenty-three young men.
Francis, the Curé's brother, complained, "I am
no longer master in my own house." However, the
inhabitants of Dardilly were delighted with their
saint, and a delegation said to him, "Make up
your mind to live here in retirement." But to satisfy
his people from Ars, the Curé had to receive faculties from the Diocese of Lyons in order to return
once again to his work of confessor—this time,
in the home town church. Ars had moved to
Dardilly.

On Saturday night, the Bishop's answer arrived:
the Curé was offered the chaplaincy of Notre-
Dame de Beaumont, a rustic little sanctuary of
Our Lady. But he was to weigh the offer care-
fully. On Tuesday, the Curé offered Mass at the
sanctuary; his intention: to obtain the light and
guidance of the Holy Ghost. After Mass, Father
Raymond asked, "Well, what is your decision?"

"The good God does not want me here," replied the Curé.

"Well, where do you wish to go?"

"Let us return to Ars."

How quickly the news was carried to Ars. The bells pealed out. The men came in from the fields. "The Curé is coming back!" The whole town assembled. Towards five o'clock, the Curé of Ars appeared. He looked at his people, whom he loved, and so overcome was he with emotion that he could only say to them, "I shall never leave you again! I shall never leave you again!" This promise he kept for ten years.

On July 25, 1852, kind Bishop Devie died. The Curé of Ars now believed that the way was open for him to flee from Ars. On September 1 of the following year, he confided to Catherine Lassagne, "I have been thinking that this time I must go." Poor Catherine! In her grief, she told Marie Filliat; and they both told Brother Jerome; he told Brother Athanase; he in turn told the new assistant, Father Toccanier. On Sunday night as he prepared to leave Ars, the Curé entrusted Catherine with a letter for the new Bishop. As he stealthily stole down the stairs of the rectory, he met a delegation. "You have sold me," he reprimanded Catherine; and the girl burst into tears.

What a sad night that Sunday night was in Ars! The Curé was leaving them! They took his Breviary from him with the hope of discouraging him, but the Curé returned to the rectory for another set. They rang the church bells in the middle of the night; and pilgrims, lodging for the night in the lobby of the bell tower, arose and joined the procession—but all seemed in vain.

"Father, before you go, hear me!"

"Let me finish my confession!"

"Oh no, kind Father, do not forsake us!"

"What! Father Vianney," remonstrated the assistant, "you who know by heart the Lives of the Saints—have you forgotten the zeal of St. Martin? Having the crown already within his grasp, did he not exclaim, 'I do not refuse to work'? Will you leave the field of battle?"

"Let us go to the church!" meekly said the Curé. The tide of battle seemed to be shifting. The Curé entered the church first. Face buried in hands, he prayed long; then putting on his surplice he went to the confessional. Afterwards, he offered Holy Mass. In the meantime the Vicar General arrived, and his words were final: it was the definite wish of the new Bishop that the Curé of Ars remain at his post. The only protest the Curé made was, "I behaved like a child."

Of this strange incident, Henri Gheon concludes: "Never in M. Vianney's life was the fiend's occult influence so clearly shown; never was it so near to a great triumph. It is the lot of saints, by God's will, to be suddenly borne to the very edge of the abyss by the same Satan who bore Our Lord to the high mountain and on to the pinnacle of the Temple." (*The Secret of the Curé D' Ars*, Henri Gheon, p. 195).

CHAPTER 18

Schedule

EXCEPT FOR his annual retreat and his so-called rest at home in 1843, from the year 1830 the Curé of Ars never left his parish. He served his God and his people by means of the sublime monotony of routine. His routine could perhaps be confined to a schedule something like this.

One hour after midnight, the Curé rang the Angelus bell and announced to the people that the church was open and that the pastor was at their disposal. Only the confessions of women were heard at this hour. As pilgrims flocked into the church, they found the Curé kneeling before the Blessed Sacrament and awaiting his penitents. Sometimes after hearing a confession, he would say with fatherly affection, "Come now, my little one, go and take your rest. You are very sleepy."

Confessions over at six o'clock, the Curé knelt on the stones of the chancel to prepare himself for Holy Mass. With hands folded and eyes fixed on the tabernacle, he remained immovable. Oh! how beautifully he offered the Holy Sacrifice! The spectacle of the Curé offering Holy Mass converted more than one sinner. Yet he took no more time than other priests. Afterwards he made his thanksgiving—with the people crowding around and staring at him. Was he not distracted? No, because he himself once said, "Flies do not settle on boiling water; they only fall into cold or tepid water." Thanksgiving over—if it were ever over for him—he blessed articles, comforted the afflicted and spoke to this one or that one crowding around to see him.

The Curé took breakfast at eight: half a glass of milk—and this in holy obedience to both Bishop and doctor. But it gave him a chance to relax over in the Providence and to see his little ones.

Returning to the sacristy at eight-thirty, the Curé heard the confessions of men.

Pausing at ten o'clock, he recited the Little Hours of the Divine Office. "When I think of those beautiful prayers," he once remarked, "I am tempted to cry out, 'Happy Fault!' For if David had had no sins to lament, we should be without them." Then more confessions.

At eleven o'clock the Curé gave his famous catechism lessons in which his tears preached stronger than his words. Not having time to prepare, he made a novena to the Holy Ghost for the special grace to speak without preparation. Inspiration took the place of preparation. He repeated himself; yet his message was always full of grace, fresh, and moving.

The Angelus was recited at noon and then the *procession* started back to the rectory. To make his way through the double line of pilgrims took fifteen minutes.

"Good Father!"

"Holy Father!"

"Bless me!"

"Pray for our sick!"

"Cure this poor little one!"

"Convert my father. . . my husband!"

The Curé would sometimes throw a handful of medals into the crowd, and during the scramble he would rush into the rectory and lock the door. Alone for a time! In the rectory there was lunch, which he always took standing. "It has happened that between noon and one o'clock," the Curé once told Brother Athanase, "I have been able to dine, sweep my room, shave, take a siesta, and visit my sick people."

A half hour later, the Curé was in the habit of leaving the rectory for his visits to the sick. Again, there was the *procession*. Sometimes priests went along with him to be edified by his gentle care for the sick. At times, people became almost rude in their efforts to obtain relics of a "living saint." They snipped parts of his cassock or surplice; they even plucked locks of his hair. They grabbed his breviary, snatched a few holy cards and then returned it—sometimes by mail, sometimes not at all. But the Curé took it all in good humor. To one lady who wanted some relics, "Go and make some yourself!"

About one-thirty, the Curé recited Vespers and Compline back in the church; a half hour later he began to hear confessions of women in the confessional; towards the close of the afternoon, about five o'clock, he heard the confessions of men in the sacristy; and finally, at eight o'clock (without supper) the poor Curé went into the pulpit and recited the little chaplet of the Immaculate Conception and night prayers.

From eight-thirty on, the schedule is uncertain. Was it suppertime? Probably there was no suppertime in the Curé's rectory. Back in the rectory, there were many interviews to be made with fellow priests, missionaries, Brothers, Sisters, and lay people. Besides, it was necessary at this time for the Curé to anticipate Matins and Lauds, and also to feed upon a few pages of spiritual reading from the Lives of Saints. What about his meditation? Before the pilgrimages, he was often found in church making his meditation. But after the pilgrimages, he once told a fellow priest: "I no longer have time for regular prayer. But at the very first moment of the day, I endeavor to unite myself closely to Jesus Christ, and I then perform my task with the thought of this union in mind."

Perhaps when the clock struck ten, the Curé was alone in the peace of his room. More probably he was back in church hearing confessions. Maybe he was still holding interviews. However, before retiring—whenever that was—there was the discipline; after retiring, there was the *grappin*, together with an open sore on his arm, his rheumatism, headaches, toothaches, double hernia, and all those pains and aches from which his poor body was never free. Besides, his bed was hard—and the floor was still harder. And remember: the Curé was due back in church at one o'clock.

Someone remarked, "We were wont to have a chapter of the Lives of the Saints enacted before our eyes, day by day."

In 1845 the Bishop sent an assistant priest to the Curé of Ars. However, the presence of an assistant made but few changes in the daily schedule of the pastor. For eight years, until 1853, the Curé had as his assistant Father Raymond, whom he loved dearly because "He is not afraid to tell me the truth about myself!"

In the hearts of the people of Ars, Father Raymond was considered as one "having been sent by God to try the patience of His faithful servant." He was twenty years younger than the Curé, and greatly indebted to him for having paid his seminary fees. Father Raymond was brilliant and very efficient, but lacking in judgment and humility. He looked upon himself as guardian rather than assistant, and with this attitude, took over the Curé's bedroom until the people complained. He always signed himself: Father Raymond, Pastor. His goal was to direct the pilgrimages and to put order and system into the crowds. In his determination, he even went so far as to take the Curé to task when he thought it necessary, and even to contradict him publicly in the pulpit. In a word, his goal was *efficiency*. "If he is made to suffer," the Curé said of Father Raymond, "we shall go away together." Certainly this assistant helped to develop to heroic stature the great virtues of humility and patience in the soul of the Curé. He was truly an instrument of God in forming a saint. To his Bishop, the Curé wrote, "I have nothing special to tell your Lordship concerning Father Raymond except that he deserves a warm place in your heart in return for all his goodness to me."

However, the situation was becoming too much for the people of Ars to bear. They insisted that their good Curé write the Bishop. Very well! The letter was dictated to Brother Athanase. The Curé read it over. He thought a moment—he tore the letter in pieces. "I was thinking," he said, "that Our Lord carried His cross. Surely I can do as He did."

In time, Father Raymond began to realize that the people wanted the *holiness* of the pastor and not the efficiency of the assistant. He loved his pastor. In fact he later began to write his life. But to take the Curé's place. . . that was another question. So he asked for a change, and the Bishop sent him to Polliat. "I have only one regret," he said later, "and that is that I did not draw more profit from his example. Nevertheless, I trust in the tender and fatherly affection that he always showed to me." Father Raymond will ever be remembered as a powerful instrument in the saintly formation of the Curé of Ars.

CHAPTER 19

Death

DID the people of France appreciate their living saint? Truly he was the best-known priest in the country. Even the popularity of the eloquent Dominican, Father Lacordaire of Paris, who visited the Curé incognito on May 3, 1845, could not eclipse that of the saintly Curé of Ars. "Here comes the saint!" the people would exclaim. Realizing that such an acclamation was the most noble possible, Bishop Devie thought it superfluous to honor the Curé by making him a canon of the cathedral. But his successor thought differently.

Three months after his enthronement, Bishop Chalandon made a visit to Ars. It was Monday, October 25, 1852, and Father Vianney was hearing confessions. The Curé hurried through the ranks of pilgrims to greet his new Bishop—and then he spied something: it was silk and red and bordered with ermine. "No, Bishop," the Curé protested. But in vain! To the singing of the *Veni Creator* the Bishop clothed him with the mozetta, the insignia of an honorary canon. Ten days later, the Curé wrote, "Bishop, the mozetta which you have had the great charity to bestow on me has given me much pleasure, because, being in want of money to complete a foundation, I have sold it for fifty francs. That price completely satisfied me."

Then the government wanted to do something to honor a citizen who was truly a public benefactor. Therefore, on August 15, 1855, the Curé of Ars was raised to the rank of a Knight of the Imperial Order of the Legion of Honor.

"Does it mean money for my poor?" asked the Curé.

"No!" answered the mayor. "It is just a distinction."

"Very well," said the Curé without hesitation. "Since the poor have nothing to gain by it, tell the Emperor, please, that I do not want it."

An artist came to paint his portrait. The Curé said laughingly, "I advise you to paint me with my mozetta and my cross of honor, and write underneath: 'Nothingness! Pride!'" The artist went away disappointed, and the Curé went on hearing his confessions.

The Curé of Ars was truly humble. He used to warn his assistant, "Humility is to the various virtues what the chain is in a rosary: take away the chain and the beads are scattered: remove humility, and all virtues vanish."

A story he never tired telling was about St. Macarius. The devil one day appeared to the saint. "All that you do, I do likewise," Satan said to the solitary of the Thebaid. "You fast; I never eat at all. You watch; I never sleep. There is only one thing you do that I am unable to perform."

"And what is that?" warily asked the saint.

"To humble myself."

The Curé sought no honors. That was the miracle of his life. He was ever in the Presence of God. What more could he want? Besides, he had probably been frequently honored with the visible presence of Our Lady. "People would not dare to set foot on such and such a flagstone in this room if they knew what took place there!" he once said to a friend. He was probably referring to the famous vision of Our Lady which he is said to have had on May 8, 1840. In the last days of his life, his new assistant, Father Toccanier, questioned the Curé about his visions. "Yes," he confided, "near the head of my bed I once saw someone dressed in white, who spoke softly to me, like a confessor." For the Curé of Ars, those were honors the world could never equal.

In the last year of his life, an old-time friend, the holy and apostolic Pauline Jaricot, visited him. Providence seemed to have abandoned her at this period of life, leaving her in a pitiable and impoverished condition. No doubt this was the price she had to pay to win the blessings of God in the years to come for the great society she inspired—The Propagation of the Faith. The good Curé, touched by her destitution, tried to make her comfortable as well as comfort her. "I beseech you," Pauline pleaded, "do not think of the cold. I am used to it. It will be much better if you warm my soul with a few sparks of faith and hope." His visit with her was short. Pilgrims were coming. Thousands of them! They feared the Curé's life was near its end, and they longed at least to see, to touch, to hear him—possibly to speak with him and receive from him absolution before the end. So the Curé blessed Pauline, gave her a wooden cross as a silent symbol of resignation, and returned to his post in the confessional.

The summer of 1859 in Ars was stifling. The hot July air in the little church seemed thick and sour from the crowds that gathered—for a last time, because they knew the Curé's time was short. The Curé suffered cruelly; he had fainted several times, and yet, the people came. "Ah," he said in his faint whisper, "sinners will kill the sinner." He was now over seventy-three years old, having spent forty-one years at Ars.

Friday, July 29, 1859, was Father Vianney's last day of full duty as the parish priest of Ars. He was faithful to duty to the end because he once said, "I know not whether I have properly discharged my duty...Oh, how I fear death! Ah! I am a great sinner!" At one o'clock in the morning, as usual, he went to his post in the confessional. The confessions were endless, and the air in the church seemed to be on fire. Over and over again, attacks of suffocation seized him; fever, burning and burning again, compelled him to leave the church—but for only a moment's rest.

At eleven o'clock he gave his catechism lesson. No one heard him, but everyone knew he was preaching on his favorite subject: love for Jesus in the Blessed Sacrament, because he kept turning to the tabernacle, weeping as he preached—preaching with his eyes more than with his lips. Then back again to the confessional. There he spent the afternoon and the evening; and when the hour was late, fully worn out, and leaning on the arm of Brother Jerome, he left his little church. He left the altar, his pulpit, his confessional, his dear Philomena and all his saintly friends: Our Lady and St. Joseph, and trudged wearily back to his rectory—never again to return.

On Saturday, July 30, the Curé of Ars did not rise from his bed. One o'clock came, but there was no Curé in church. He called for someone, and faithful Catherine Lassagne hurried in. "It is my poor end," the Curé whispered. "Go and call my confessor."

"I shall send for the doctor," said Catherine.

"It is useless. The doctor can do nothing."

"St. Philomena will cure you," hopefully suggested the weeping Father Toccanier.

"Oh," sighed the Curé, "St. Philomena can do nothing now!"

This time, in his last hour, the enemy was not permitted to tempt the poor Curé. He did not seem to suffer as he did in 1843. All seemed so peaceful! Even the horrible fear of death that had beset him his whole life long had vanished. "How sweet it is to die," he once had said, "if one has lived on the cross!"

Soon Father Beau, his faithful confessor for over

thirteen years, arrived and heard his last confession. Dr. Saunier, who had treated him in 1843, came; and there also came a Sister of St. Joseph who brushed away the flies from his face, bathed in perspiration. "Leave me with my poor flies," he seemed to say; "the only thing that worries me is sin." All his dear friends gathered: Catherine, who was ever loyal; his good teaching Brothers, Athanase and Jerome; his beloved assistant, Father Toccanier; the members of the des Garets family, to whom he had been a father; his penitents, parishioners, and pilgrims. They forced their way into his room. "He was our parish priest before he became yours," they argued with Brother Athanase who was acting as guard as they poured into the room. Those who could not enter knelt outside. Now and then a small bell tinkled. It told them that someone was lifting the Curé's arm in blessing.

On Tuesday, August 2, Father Beau made his way through the weeping crowd as he carried Holy Viaticum to his saintly penitent. Some twenty priests walked in procession carrying lighted tapers. "How kind the good God is," murmured the Curé. "When we are no longer able to go to Him, He Himself comes to us!" Having hoped against hope that St. Philomena would miraculously intervene for the cure of her cherished priest, Father Beau had put off Extreme Unction. Finally, the Curé had insisted on the Last Sacraments. He received them with the faith of a saint.

As he lingered on, someone broached the subject of his place of burial. Weak as he was, on Wednesday the Curé was approached. "At Ars. . .," he whispered. ". . .my body is not much."

His Bishop came, embraced him but said little. Father Vianney smiled. At ten o'clock that night, his assistant gave him the apostolic blessing and the plenary indulgence. By midnight, the fast-failing Curé still had strength to recite the prayers for the dying. He kissed the missionary cross fervently and grasped it firmly as he waited for His beloved Master.

Thursday, August 4, 1859, came. Conscious and at peace, the Curé rested in the arms of Brother Jerome. Each minute, each second seemed his last. At two o'clock, worn out, he who had borne the burden of the day's heat, even from the first hour in the Master's vineyard, fell asleep. Worthy of his hire, John Marie Vianney, the Curé of Ars was born in Heaven.

CHAPTER 20

Glory

IN THE WORLD beyond, those penances—
those terrible penances—were meriting their
glory; but in the world of Ars, those penances
had left a body—"my poor corpse"—a mass of
wounds and sores. The Curé of Ars had begged
that no one undress him after death. He wished
to conceal from the eyes of men the penances he
had inflicted on his body for the souls of men.
But the missionaries and the Brothers had to deny
his request; at five in the morning, they had their
spiritual father vested in cassock, surplice, and
stole and had him laid in state on the first floor
of the rectory. For the first time, the Curé had
to submit to a photographer. Then an unending
procession of the Curé's children began. As they
passed the bier in reverential love, they had time
only for an Our Father and Hail Mary, so pressing was the throng. At their insistence, the religious Brothers touched the devotional effects of
the poor people to the precious relics of their pastor and confessor.

Saturday, August 6, 1859, was the day of the
funeral. Three hundred priests and over six thousand people were present. As the body was carried

from the rectory to the church, the procession seemed not so much a funeral procession as a gloriously triumphal one. The whole village became a church: the people, hearing the sanctus bell, knelt in the streets, in the square, in the cemetery—wherever they found themselves. In the distance the knell of the neighboring church bells could be heard, paying their respects to the memory of the beloved Curé of Ars. After the absolution, the casket was placed in the Chapel of St. John the Baptist in front of the empty confessional. On August 14, the remains were lowered into a vault constructed in the middle of the church. The tomb was closed by a marble slab inscribed with the words: "Here lies John Marie Baptist Vianney, the Curé of Ars."

Before long, the ardent kisses of countless pilgrims wore away the marble inscription. In life, pilgrims swarmed to the confessional box of the Curé; in death, they deluged his tomb. Because the voice of the people is often the voice of God, the diocesan authorities were constrained to open the process of Father Vianney. On October 3, 1872, Pope Pius IX declared the Curé of Ars "Venerable." His successor, Pope Leo XIII, said to the postulator of the cause: "This Cause surpasses all others. It must suffer no delay. I greatly desire to beatify the Venerable Vianney."

This consolation of declaring the Curé "Blessed," however, was given to the parish priest of Tombolo and Salzano, St. Pius X. "Nothing more agreeable, nothing more profitable could have happened," the saintly Pontiff said to some members of the French clergy, "not only to us, who for so many years have gladly carried out the duties of the parochial ministry, but to the parish priests of the whole world, than to see this Venerable Curé invested with the honor of the Blessed, the more so that his glory will be reflected upon all those whose life is dedicated to the care of souls." On Sunday morning, January 8, 1905, in the Eternal City, the humble Curé of Ars was declared "Blessed" to the resounding strains of the *Te Deum* intoned by the thunderous voices of thirty thousand people.

Three months later, on April 12, 1905, St. Pius X decreed the Curé of Ars "the patron of all priests having the care of souls in France and in the countries subject to France." On the desk of St. Pius X was a statue of his dearly beloved, Blessed John Marie. "He is my companion—*socius meus*," said the Pope once to a friend. "Let us pray God to work, as soon as possible, by his intercession, the miracles that will allow us to canonize him."

Many years later, on December 20, 1935, Pope Pius XI in his great encyclical on the Catholic Priesthood said that it was the Curé of Ars "whom we have willed to set up before *all parish priests* as their model and heavenly Patron."

Back in Ars, a beautiful church, which the holy Curé had only envisioned, was built and completed by 1895. In the transept of the great church, the holy remains of the Curé of Ars were placed in a reliquary of bronze—the church's most prized relic.

During the pontificate of Pope Benedict XV, the two miracles required for the canonization of Blessed John Marie were examined and found worthy to sanction the glorious honor of canonization.

On the feast of Pentecost, May 31, 1925, two weeks after the magnificent splendors that surrounded the canonization of St. Thérèse of the Child Jesus, the glorious honors of sainthood were conferred on the Curé of Ars. He who had matched in life the sanctity of little Thérèse, shared her triumph in death. Theresian crowds had remained in the Eternal City to witness the triumph of that priesthood to sanctify which Thérèse had dedicated her life; the same purple and gold hangings, used at her canonization, still adorned the vast interior of St. Peter's; the same silver trumpets stood ready to peal forth the glorious proclamation.

At half past ten in the morning, silence swept through the milling throngs. Surrounded by a galaxy of thirty-five Cardinals and over two hundred mitred Bishops, Pope Pius XI, as Head of the Universal Church and unerring Teacher of all, broke the silence with the infallible and blessed words:

"WE DECLARE

TO BE A SAINT

AND WE ENROLL

IN THE CATALOGUE OF THE SAINTS

THE BLESSED

JOHN MARIE BAPTIST VIANNEY."

Then the vast throngs erupted with shouts of joy; then the trumpets blared; then the bells burst out in merry song—the beautiful bells of Rome— each bell seeming to sing:

THANKS BE TO GOD
AND HIS MOTHER MARY.

BIBLIOGRAPHY

THE CURÉ D'ARS: ST. JEAN-MARIE-BAPTISTE VIANNEY
  By Abbé Francis Trochu
  TAN Books and Publishers, Inc.
  Rockford, Illinois

LIFE OF THE CURÉ D'ARS
  By Abbé Alfred Monnin
  Kelly, Piet and Company
  Baltimore, Maryland

THE SECRET OF THE CURÉ D'ARS
  By Henri Gheon
  Sheed and Ward
  New York City

LITTLE CATECHISM OF THE CURÉ OF ARS
  (formerly titled *The Curé of Ars to His People*)
  TAN Books and Publishers, Inc.
  Rockford, Illinois

LE CURÉ D'ARS
  By Abbé Francis Trochu
  Le Livre Chretien, Librairie Artheme Fayard
  Paris, France

THE PARISH PRIEST OF ARS
By Mary Fabyan Windeatt
Grail Publications
Saint Meinrad, Indiana

SAINTS FOR NOW
Edited by Clare Boothe Luce
"The Curé of Ars," by Bruce Marshall
Sheed and Ward
New York City

PARISH PRIESTS AMONG THE SAINTS
Rev. Walter Gumbley, O.P.
The Newman Bookshop
Westminster, Maryland

ANNALES D'ARS
Organe Du Pelerinage D'Ars
Ars, Formans, France

Thomas Nelson

A view of Ars as one approaches by road from the east. The terrain consists of gently rolling hills, and most of the environs are under cultivation.

Thomas Nelson

The Basilica of Ars as seen from the main street when approaching from the west.

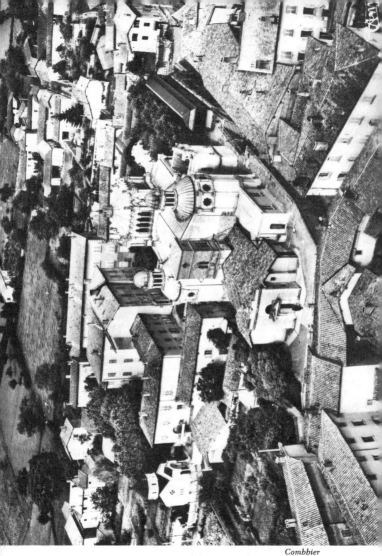

An aerial view of Ars, with the Basilica just to the right
of center. The low portion of the building is the original
parish church of the Curé of Ars, though even this was gradually expanded over the years of his ministry.

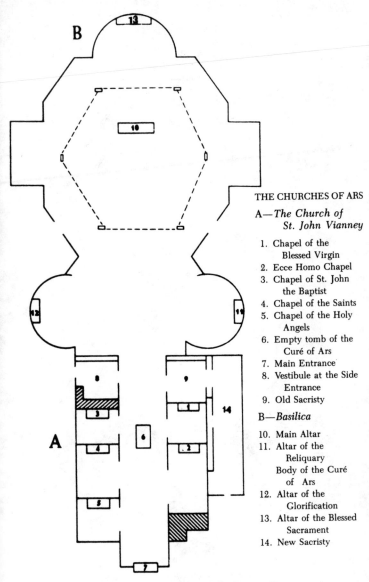

THE CHURCHES OF ARS

A—*The Church of St. John Vianney*

1. Chapel of the Blessed Virgin
2. Ecce Homo Chapel
3. Chapel of St. John the Baptist
4. Chapel of the Saints
5. Chapel of the Holy Angels
6. Empty tomb of the Curé of Ars
7. Main Entrance
8. Vestibule at the Side Entrance
9. Old Sacristy

B—*Basilica*

10. Main Altar
11. Altar of the Reliquary Body of the Curé of Ars
12. Altar of the Glorification
13. Altar of the Blessed Sacrament
14. New Sacristy

Editions Lescuyer et Fils, Lyon, France

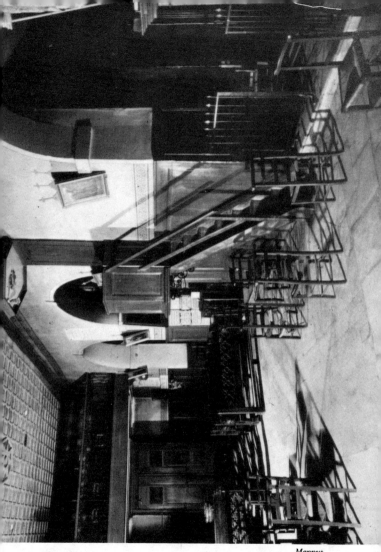

The interior of the parish church of Ars, looking back toward the main entrance. On the right is the Curé's pulpit. The three arches enter into small chapels off the main church.

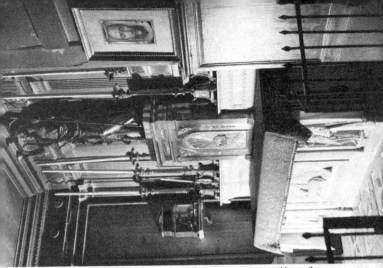

Mappus/Lescuyer

Trochu/Lescuyer

Above: The Chapel of St. John the Baptist.
Below: The Chapel of the Holy Angels.

Trochu/Lescuyer

Thomas Nelson

Above: The Chapel of St. Philomena, to whom St. John Vianney was especially devoted and to whom he ascribed all the miracles worked at Ars.
Below: The Chapel of the Blessed Virgin Mary, Our Lady of Ars.

Above: The confessional where St. John Vianney heard the confessions of the women, located in the Chapel of St. John the Baptist, to whom the holy Curé was especially devoted. *Below:* The confessional where he heard the men's confessions. It is located in the old sacristy.

The shrine holding the incorrupt body of St. John Vianney, viewed from across the nave of the Basilica portion of the church at Ars.

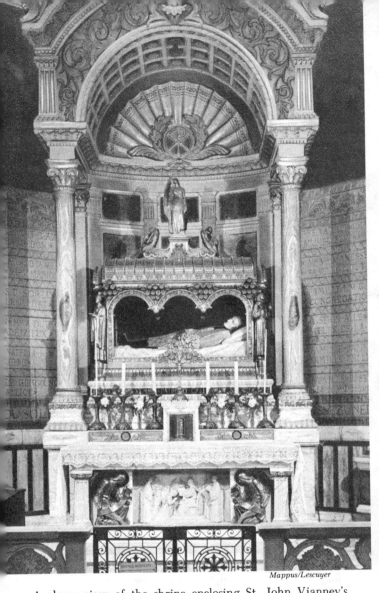

Mappus/Lescuyer

A closer view of the shrine enclosing St. John Vianney's incorrupt body.

A close-up view of the Curé's incorrupt body. The face is actually a mask.

Trochu/Lescuyer

The main altar of the Basilica as it formerly appeared.

The main altar of the Basilica as it appears today.

Thomas Nelson

The Chapel of the Heart, viewed from the Basilica. Here reposes the heart of St. John Vianney, removed from his body in 1905, the year of his beatification. Also contained in this chapel is the famous statue of the Saint on his knees in prayer, rendered by Cabuchet.

SAINT CURÉ D'ARS PROTÉGEZ LE CHEF DE L'EGLISE ET TOUS LES CURÉS DE L'UNIVERS

Interior of the Chapel of the Heart. The Curé's heart is in the reliquary above the famous kneeling statue and between the two angels.

The garden of the rectory from which one enters the Curé's house.

Mappus/Lescuyer

The kitchen of the Curé where he would boil his potatoes.

The room of the Curé of Ars, much as it appears today.

Mappus/Lescuyer

The library of the Curé of Ars located in his room opposite the foot of his bed. Though he had but two years' formal education when he began studies for the priesthood, the Curé of Ars was well read in the Faith, as his large library of well-worn books attests.

La Crypte, the modern subterranean church at Ars built to accommodate for Mass the huge crowds of pilgrims (over 500,000 come each year), and constructed below ground to preserve the flavor of the original town. *La Crypte* holds easily 1,500 persons for Mass.

Thomas Nelson

View of the top of *La Crypte* looking away to the south from the yard of the Basilica. Without having it pointed out to him, the traveller would never realize it is there.

Chapel and house of *La Providence*, where Catherine Lassagne conducted, under the auspices of the Curé of Ars, a small orphanage.

Trochu/Lescuyer

Ars—still very much the small farming town it was in the
days of the holy Curé.

Two outstanding Catholic books...

THE CURÉ OF ARS—PATRON SAINT OF PARISH PRIESTS. Fr. Bartholomew O'Brien.

Special Quantity Discount

1 copy	4.50	
5 copies	3.00 each	15.00 total
10 copies	2.50 each	25.00 total
25 copies	2.25 each	56.25 total
50 copies	2.00 each	100.00 total
100 copies	1.75 each	175.00 total
500 copies	1.50 each	750.00 total

Priced low purposely for wide distribution.

THE LITTLE CATECHISM OF THE CURÉ OF ARS. St. John Vianney. Here is Catholic wisdom stated in a simple, sublime and penetrating way and found nowhere else but in the words of the Curé of Ars. Divided into 36 short chapters, *The Little Catechism* covers every basic aspect of our spiritual struggle. An incomparable description of the battle we all face to save our souls and probably the simplest, most persuasive exortation ever written admonishing us to renounce our sins and lead a holy life.

Special Quantity Discount

1 copy	5.50	
5 copies	4.00 each	20.00 total
10 copies	3.50 each	35.00 total
15 copies	3.25 each	48.75 total
25 copies	3.00 each	75.00 total
50 copies	2.75 each	137.50 total
100 copies	2.50 each	250.00 total
500 copies	2.25 each	1125.00 total

Priced low purposely for wide distribution.

ORDER YOUR COPIES TODAY!